Holidays & Celebrations

How to Make Books with Children Series

Holidays and celebrations are an important part of every school year. Enhance your observations of traditional and nontraditional holidays by creating books. *How to Make Books with Children, Holiday and Celebrations* provides resources for 38 special events.

- historical background and facts about the day
- a list of fiction and nonfiction books
- step-by-step directions for a class or individual book-making project
- reproducible patterns that insure book project success

As you enjoy holiday celebrations with your students, be sure to

- connect the new learnings with students' lives by discussing their experiences
- enjoy reading and rereading the poems, stories, reports, and plays that you publish
- write new stories combining characters from different holidays just as Robin Pulver did in **The Holiday Handwriting School** (Four Winds Press, 1991).
- invent your own holiday. Explain its purpose, invent special symbols, and then celebrate!

Author: Jill Norris, Joy Evans
Illustrator: Cindy Davis
Editor: Marilyn Evans
Desktop: Cheryl Puckett

Evan-Moor
EDUCATIONAL PUBLISHERS
EMC 578

Table of Contents

Pop-Up Book Binding

Paper Cover: Pop-up books generate lots of student interest. Students love to read the stories again and again to share the excitment of seeing the pop-up revealed. Follow these steps for easy, successful binding:

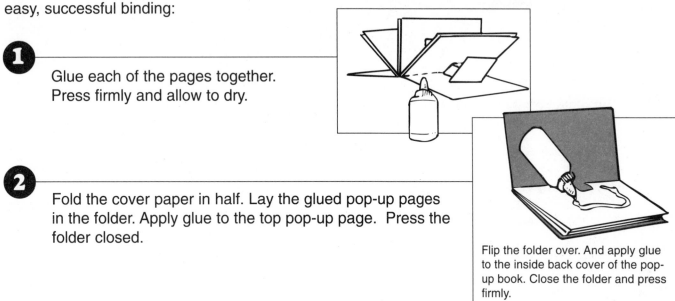

1 Glue each of the pages together. Press firmly and allow to dry.

2 Fold the cover paper in half. Lay the glued pop-up pages in the folder. Apply glue to the top pop-up page. Press the folder closed.

Flip the folder over. And apply glue to the inside back cover of the pop-up book. Close the folder and press firmly.

Cloth or Wallpaper Cover: Cardboard covered with cloth or wallpaper may be used to create sturdy and impressive covers for student pop-up books.

1 Cut two pieces of cardboard about two inches (5 cm) larger than the story pages. Place the cardboard on a piece of cloth cut slightly larger than the cover. Leave an appropriate amount of space between the cardboard pieces for the spine.

2 Miter the corners of the fabric. Brush diluted white glue onto the fabric border and fold over onto the cardboard.

3 Lay the pop-up book inside the cover. Brush glue on the top page. Close the cover and press firmly. Turn the cover over and open to apply glue to last pop-up page. Close the cover and press firmly again. Set aside to dry.

Hinged Binding

A hinged binding is appropriate if the book contains many pages and you want to use tagboard or another heavy material for the cover. The hinged book creates a book cover that opens easily and stands up to many readings.

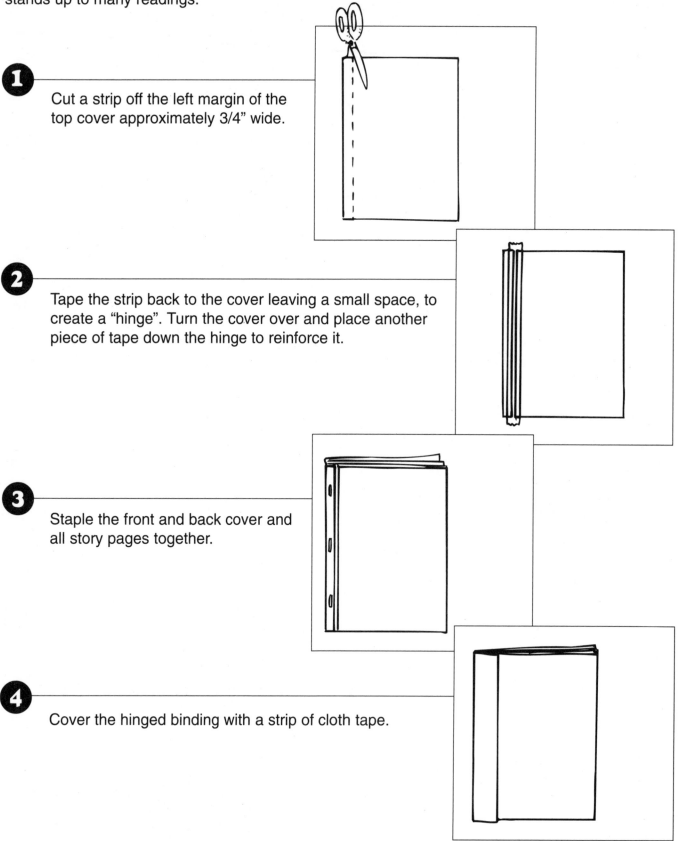

1 Cut a strip off the left margin of the top cover approximately 3/4" wide.

2 Tape the strip back to the cover leaving a small space, to create a "hinge". Turn the cover over and place another piece of tape down the hinge to reinforce it.

3 Staple the front and back cover and all story pages together.

4 Cover the hinged binding with a strip of cloth tape.

New Year's Day

January 1

Background

New Year's Day celebrations mark the end of an old year and the start of a new year. All over the world the New Year is greeted with noise. The noisy greeting at midnight is an important part of New Year's Eve. This custom goes back to an ancient belief that noise will scare away evil spirits, making room for the good spirits to come and bless the new year.

Books to Read

New Year's Magic by James Baker; Lerner Publications, 1989.

Un-happy New Year, Emma by James Stevenson; Greenwillow Books, 1989.

Where's Molly? by Uli Waas; North-South Books, 1993.

Facts

*   Julius Caesar gave the first month of the year its name in honor of Janus, Roman god of gates and doors and keeper of the gates of heaven and earth. Since most doors lead both in and out, Janus is portrayed with two faces, one looking backward to the old year, the other looking forward to the new. In his left hand, Janus is pictured as holding a scepter, a symbol of power; in his right, he holds a key with which he can close the door of the old year and open the door to the new. Since Janus was the god of all beginnings, people begin the new year by promising to be better. They make special promises called resolutions.

*   The new year symbol of the baby was used as early as the fifth century B.C. The Athenians cradled a baby in a basket and carried him in the place of honor in their ceremonial procession.

*   In England long ago, the people opened their doors at the stroke of midnight to let the old year out and the new year in.

The Popper

An Individual Student Book

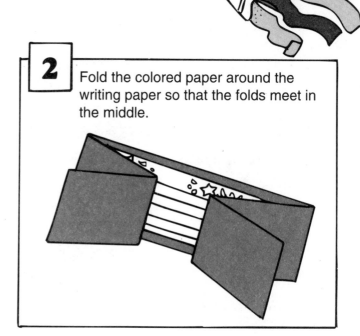

Materials

- popper pattern on page 7
- writing form on page 8
- 4" x 32" (10 x 81 cm) strip of brightly colored butcher paper
- paper strips pattern on page 8
- 4" x 12" (10 x 30.5 cm) sheet of writing paper
- felt pens or crayons
- glue and scissors

1 Glue the finished writing form in the center of the long paper strip.

2 Fold the colored paper around the writing paper so that the folds meet in the middle.

3 Glue the popper pattern on the top layer.

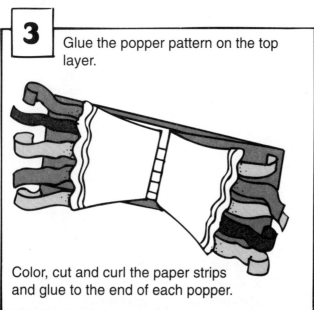

Color, cut and curl the paper strips and glue to the end of each popper.

Writing Suggestions

Write New Year's Resolutions

1. Begin by listing the things that you want to accomplish in the new year.

2. Write them in this form:

   In 2000 I'm going to be a
   book-reading,
   roller-blading,
   ice cream-licking
   third grader.

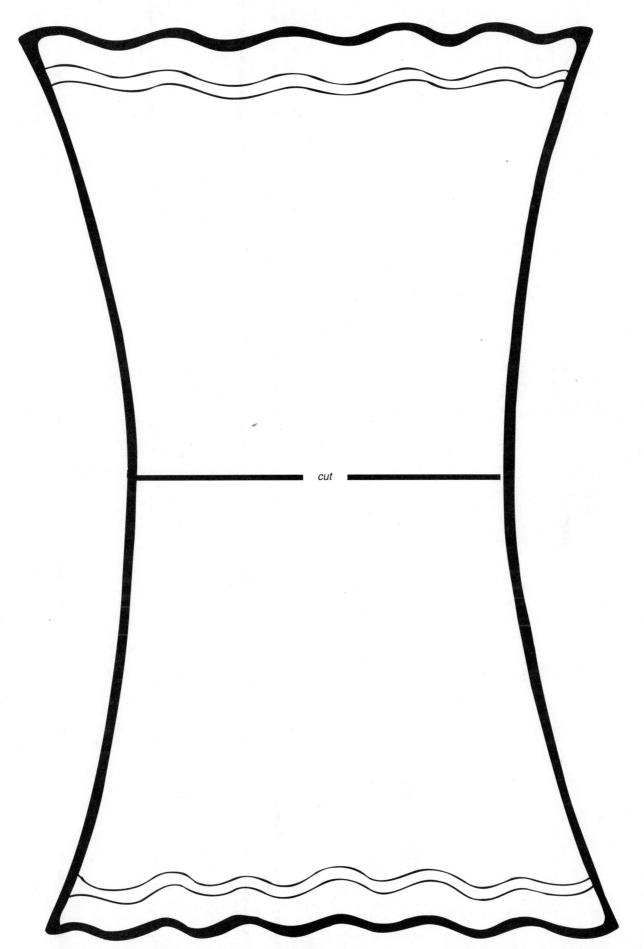

cut

Happy New Year

Martin Luther King, Jr.'s Birthday

January 15

Background

As a leader in the field of human rights, Martin Luther King, Jr. believed in bringing equality for all people through non-violent means. Martin Luther King, Jr. spoke of his dream that the United States be true to its creed that all men are created equal. In 1964 he earned the Nobel Prize for Peace. He was assassinated on April 4, 1968. His birthday, January 15, has been declared a national holiday. This is a day for Americans to dedicate themselves to the goal of equal rights for all.

Books to Read

Happy Birthday, Martin Luther King by Jean Marzollo; Scholastic, 1993.

I am Freedom's Child by Bill Martin, Jr.; Trumpet Book Club, 1987.

If You Lived at the Time of Martin Luther King by Ellen Levine; Scholastic, 1990.

I Have a Dream by Margaret Davidson; Scholastic, 1985.

Martin Luther King Day by Linda Lowery; Scholastic, 1987.

Martin Luther King, Jr. Day by Lynda Sorensen; The Rourke Press, 1994.

My Dream of Martin Luther King by Faith Ringgold; Crown Publishers, 1995.

A Picture Book of Martin Luther King, Jr. by David A. Adler; Scholastic, 1989.

Facts

- Martin Luther King, Jr. was born January 15, 1929.

- Martin finished high school two years early and entered Morehouse College in Atlanta when he was 15.

- Martin earned his doctorate from Boston University and in 1954 began his first job as pastor in Montgomery, Alabama.

- In 1963 Dr. King led the march on Washington. More than 250 thousand people joined him in Washington D.C. where he gave his famous "I Have a Dream" speech.

The Handshake

A Class Book

Materials

- hand pattern on page 11
- writing form on page 12
- 9" x 12" (23 x 35.5 cm) brown and beige construction paper
- 12" x 18" (30.5 x 45.5 cm) black construction paper
- 3" x 9" (7.5 x 23 cm) strip of white construction paper
- three paper fasteners
- scissors, glue, and black felt pen

1

Use the pattern to cut a hand from brown paper. Cut another hand from beige paper.

2

Use the felt pen to letter "I have a dream" on the white paper.

Glue the pieces together to create the cover.

3

Secure the writing papers in the folder with paper fasteners.

Writing Suggestions

Martin Luther King, Jr. dreamed that his children would live in a land where they would be recognized "not by the color of their skin, but by the content of their character." Write about your dreams for the future.

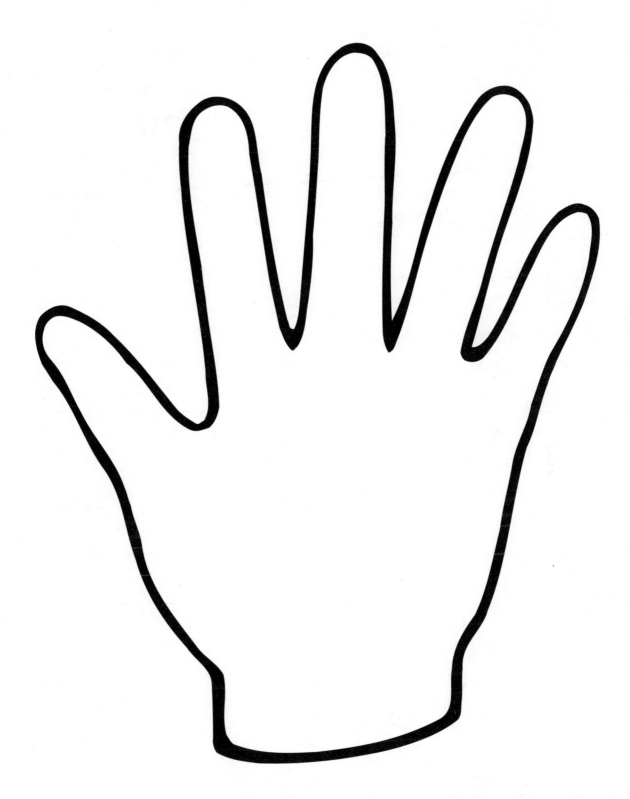

Martin
Luther
King,
Jr.

_____

_____

_____

_____

_____

_____

_____

_____

_____

Chinese New Year

The first day of the first new moon after January 21

Background

The Chinese calendar is different from the Gregorian calendar that is used in the United States. Invented by Emperor Huang-Ti, it has a 12 year cycle. The Chinese New Year occurs on the first day of the first new moon after January 21.

To get ready for the new year, families clean their houses from top to bottom. They put away sharp things like scissors and knives so that nothing will "cut" the luck of the new year. People wear new clothes and shoes to begin the year. New Year's wishes are written on long scrolls and hung in windows.

The celebration climaxes with a parade led by a long dragon. People hold up the dragon and make it dance and weave through the streets. The dragon dance is believed to chase away bad luck. Firecrackers explode as the dragon passes.

Books to Read

The Cable Car and the Dragon by Herb Caen; Doubleday, 1972.

Chinese New Year by Dianne MacMillan; Enslow Publishers, 1994.

Chinese New Year by Tricia Brown; Henry Holt & Co., 1987.

Gung Hay Fat Choy by June York Behrens; Children's Press, 1982.

Lion Dancer by Kate Waters and Madeline Slovenz-Low; Scholastic, 1990.

Facts

- Each year in the twelve–year cycle is named for one of the twelve animals that visited the bedside of the dying Buddha: rat, ox, tiger, hare, dragon, snake, horse, ram, monkey, rooster, dog, and boar. The animals are said to influence the personality and fortunes of the people born in that year.

Year of the:

Rat	1972, 1984, 1996
Ox	1973, 1985, 1997
Tiger	1974, 1986, 1998
Hare	1975, 1987, 1999
Dragon	1976, 1988, 2000
Snake	1977, 1989, 2001
Horse	1978, 1990, 2002
Ram	1979, 1991, 2003
Monkey	1980, 1992, 2004
Rooster	1981, 1993, 2005
Dog	1982, 1994, 2006
Boar	1983, 1995, 2007

The Year of the ____

A Class Book

Materials

- patterns on pages 15 and 16
- 9" x 12" (23 x 30.5 cm) red construction paper
- 4" x 8" (10 x 20 cm) writing paper
- paper fasteners
- scissors, glue, hole punch
- felt pens or crayons
- twine

1 Cut out the patterns. Glue the cycle of years wheel to the construction paper. Glue the writing paper below it.

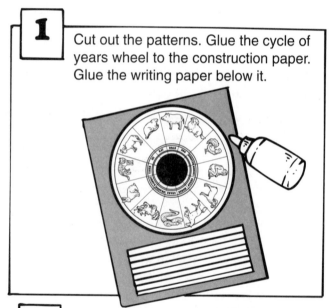

2 Cut out the window of the wheel cover. Attach with a paper fastener.

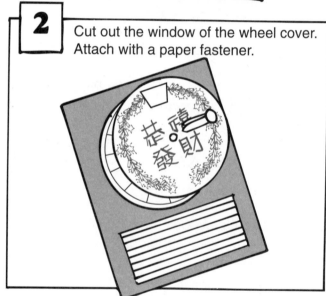

3 Place student pages together and punch holes to bind. Tie with twine.

Glue the Happy New Year symbols on the cover.

Writing Suggestions

The Chinese people believe that if you are born in the Year of the Monkey, your life will be influenced by the monkey's special qualities. Brainstorm the qualities of the animals that stand for the birth years of your students. Have individual students write about how they are like their animal.

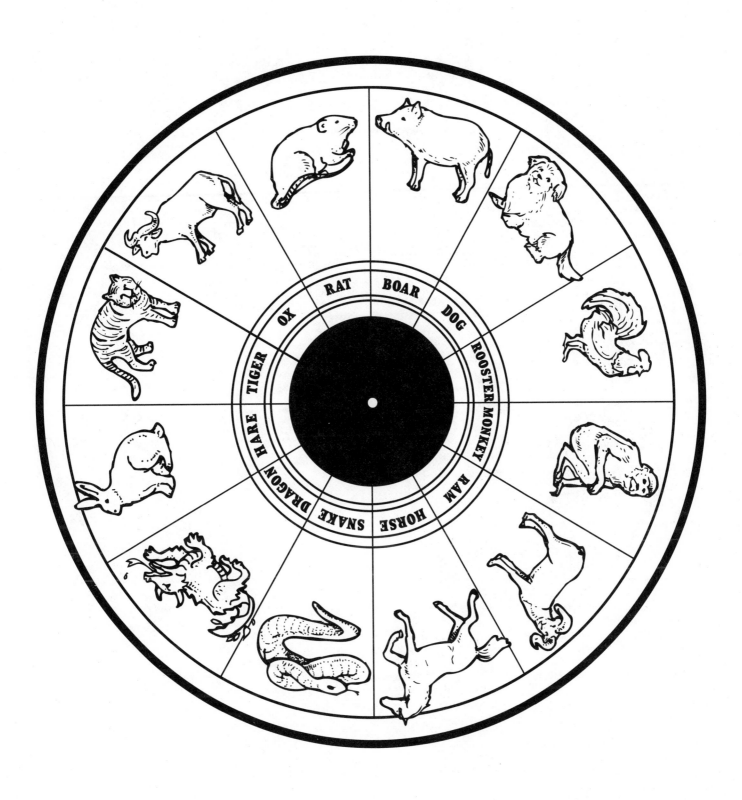

15

How to Make Books with Children EMC 578

The Chinese symbols above are pronounced Gung Hay Fat Choy - Happy New Year

Groundhog Day

February 2

Background

On February 2, tradition says that groundhogs come out of their holes in the ground and tell the world whether there will be an early or a late spring. If the groundhog comes out of his winter burrow and sees his shadow, he will run back into his burrow and winter will last another six weeks. However, if the day is cloudy, the groundhog will not see his shadow and will stay outside in anticipation of an early spring.

The groundhog is an American tradition. In Germany, badgers "predict" the weather. When Germans settlers immigrated to America, they didn't find any badgers, so they relied on the groundhog for their spring weather forecasts.

Books to Read

Geoffrey Groundhog Predicts the Weather by Bruce Koscielniak; Houghton Mifflin, 1995.

Gertie Groundhog by Joyce Holland; T. S. Denison & Company, 1963.

It's Groundhog Day! by Steven Kroll; Scholastic, 1987.

Shadow Chaser by Stephen Cosgrove; Multnomah Press, 1987.

What Happened Today, Freddy Groundhog? by Marvin Glass; Crown Publishers, 1989.

Facts

- The National Geographic Society has tested the groundhog's accuracy over a span of sixty years. The groundhog was right only 28% of the years in the study.

- Groundhog Day is probably an extension of a Roman holiday, Candlemas. Since Candlemas Day came in midwinter, the date was often used to predict the weather for the rest of the season.
    "If Candlemas Day is fair and clear, there'll be two winters in the year."

Groundhog
An Individual Student Book

Materials

- groundhog pattern on page 19
- 2 sheets of 12" x 12" (30.5 x 30.5 cm) construction paper—one blue and one green
- 1 sheet of 4" x 8" (10 x 20 cm) black paper
- 6" (15 cm) yellow circle
- writing paper
- scissors, glue, crayons
- hole punch
- strip of yellow ribbon

1 Mark the green paper and cut a curved line. Cut the writing paper in the same shape.

2 Trace around the top of the groundhog pattern on the black paper. Cut it out .

3 Glue the yellow circle and the groundhog to the blue paper. Glue the black "shadow" to the green paper.

Punch holes on the left side and secure with the ribbon.

Writing Suggestions

Write from the perspective of a groundhog. Imagine:

What happened when you poked your head above the ground after a cold winter underground?

What did you see?

What happened because of what you did?

How to Make Books with Children EMC 578

How to Make Books with Children EMC 578

Lincoln's Birthday

February 12

Background

Abraham Lincoln, the sixteenth president of the United States, is remembered for his Emancipation Proclamation, which declared slavery illegal. "Honest Abe" was a self-made man who grew up in a log cabin and read books by firelight. During Lincoln's term in office, the Civil War started and ended. During the war Lincoln went to Gettysburg, Pennsylvania, to dedicate a soldier's cemetery. There he gave his famous Gettysburg Address. He was assassinated in 1865, just five days after the South surrendered, ending the war.

Books to Read

The Gettysburg Address by Abraham Lincoln; Houghton Mifflin, 1995.

If You Grew Up with Abraham Lincoln by Ann McGovern; Scholastic, 1992.

Just Like Abraham Lincoln by Bernard Waber; Scholastic, 1964.

Lincoln, In His Own Words edited by Milton Meltzer; Harcourt Brace, 1993.

The Long Road to Gettysburg by Jim Murphy; Clarion Books, 1992.

A Picture Book of Abraham Lincoln by David A. Adler; Trumpet Book Club, 1989.

Young Abraham Lincoln by Andrew Woods; Troll Associates, 1992.

Facts

- Abraham Lincoln was born in a log cabin beside Nolin Creek in Kentucky. The cabin had a door, one window, a chimney, and a mud floor.

- When Abe was seven, he moved with his family to the newest state in the union, Indiana.

- When Abe was eight, his mother died.

- Mr. Lincoln probably spent no more than one year of his life in a classroom. His stepmother, Sarah, valued education and encouraged his "book learning."

- When he was twenty-eight, Mr. Lincoln took his legal exams and became a lawyer.

- Lincoln sometimes carried messages or important papers in his stovepipe hat.

What's under My Hat?

A Class Book

Materials

- hat, portrait, and writing form on page 22
- 5" x 18" (13 x 18 cm) white construction paper
- 12" x 18" (30.5 x 45.5 cm) construction paper
- 7" x 9" (18 x 23 cm) writing paper
- scissors, glue
- crayons or felt pens
- 3 paper fasteners

1 Color the hat and face. Fold the white construction paper as shown. Glue the hat, writing form, and portrait as shown.

Fold paper in half. Fold the top half back.

2 Glue the writing paper to the inside left. Glue the lift-up piece to the inside right.

3 Bind student pages in a construction paper cover. Enlarge the hat pattern on page 22 and glue to cover.

Writing Suggestions

Inside Lincoln's hat have students make some notes for a speech or something that they would need to remember to do if they were president.

On the writing form at the left, write about Abraham Lincoln's life. You may want to create a timeline for student reference before you ask them to write.

     How to Make Books with Children EMC 578

What's Under My Hat?

Valentine's Day

February 14

Background

Thousands of years ago wild wolves roamed Europe. The Romans thought a special god would protect them from the wolves, so they gave a party in that god's honor every February. They noticed that on the day of the party the birds seemed to choose their mates. They decided to do the same. The unmarried girls put their names on a slip of paper and put the slips into a large jar. Each unmarried boy took a slip from the jar and read the name of the girl who would be his sweetheart. The men gave gifts to their sweethearts and wrote them love letters.

Today Valentine's Day is a time to celebrate love and friendship.

Books to Read

Arthur's Valentine by Marc Brown; Little, Brown, 1980.

Be My Valentine by M. J. Carr; Scholastic, 1992.

Four Valentines in a Rainstorm by Felicia Bond; Harper & Row, 1983.

One Zillion Valentines by Frank Modell; Trumpet Book Club, 1981.

Secret Valentine by Catherine Stock; Bradbury Press, 1991.

The Valentine Bears by Eve Bunting; Clarion Books, 1983.

Valentine Friends by Ann Schweninger; Puffin Books, 1988.

Facts

- The name given to this holiday honors two saints named Valentine. They were put to death on February 14 in the year 200 A.D.

- The first St. Valentine was killed because he continued to perform marriages after the emperor had forbidden them.

- The second St. Valentine was in jail because he helped Christians. He fell in love with the jailer's daughter, cured her blindness, and wrote her love notes signed "From your Valentine."

Fine Feathered Friend

An Individual Student Book

Materials

- pop-up form on page 25
- writing form on page 26
- 12" x 18" (30.5 x 45.5 cm) construction paper
- pink and red paper scraps
- scissors, glue
- felt pens or crayons

1 Color and cut out the pop-up bird pattern. Cut hearts to glue around the pop-up.

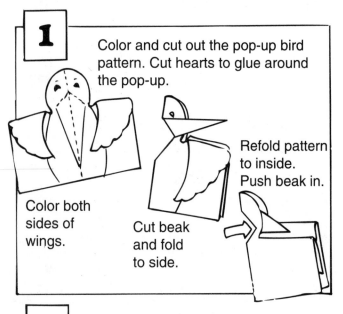

Color both sides of wings.

Cut beak and fold to side.

Refold pattern to inside. Push beak in.

2 Fold the construction paper piece in half. Glue the pop-up and the writing form into the center fold.

3 Close the folder and decorate the front with hearts. Write the title and author's name.

Writing Suggestions

As a class, brainstorm the special attributes of good friends. Write them on the hearts that surround the fine feathered friend.

Write a valentine message to a friend. Tell why the friend is special. Thank the friend for caring. Invite the friend to share a valentine treat.

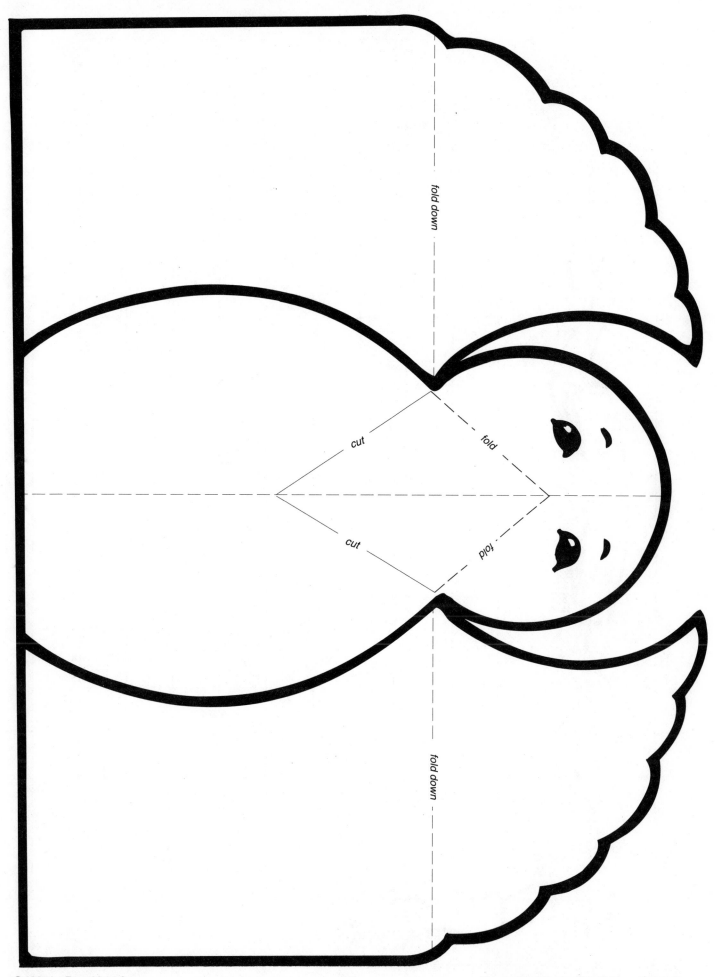

fold down

cut

fold

cut

fold

fold down

How to Make Books with Children EMC 578

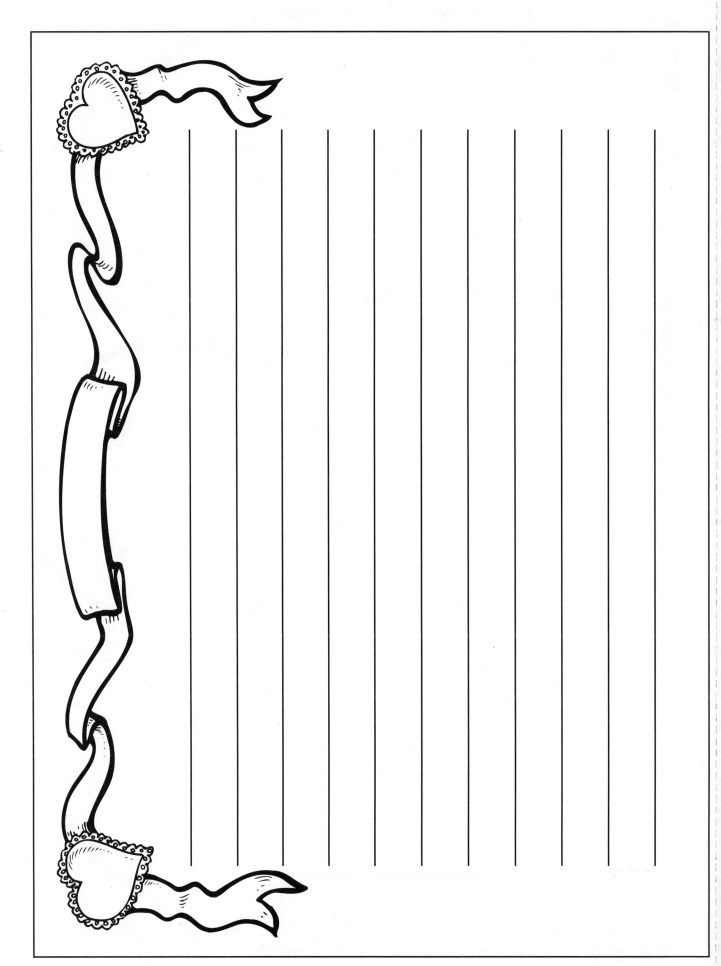

How to Make Books with Children EMC 578

Washington's Birthday

February 22

Background

George Washington, the first president of the United States, was Commander-in-Chief of the Continental Army in the Revolutionary War. He is known as the "father of the country." The first public celebration of Washington's birthday was a drum and fife concert at Valley Forge in 1778. The concert was organized by Washington's soldiers to show their appreciation for his leadership.

Books to Read

George Washington's Breakfast by Jean Fritz; Coward-McCann, 1969.

If You Grew Up with George Washington by Ruth Belov Gross; Scholastic, 1982.

The Joke's on George by Michael O. Tunnell; Tambourine Books, 1993.

Washington's Birthday by Dennis Brindell Fradin; Enslow Publishers, 1990.

Young George Washington by Andrew Woods; Troll Associates, 1992.

Facts

* George Washington was born in eastern Virginia on February 22, 1732.

* His best subject in school was math.

* George's father died when he was eleven.

* At sixteen, he became a surveyor and surveyed the Virginia wilderness for Lord Fairfax.

* He was a soldier during the French and Indian War and became the Commander of the Continental Army during the Revolutionary War.

Tri-Cornered Hat
An Individual Student Book

Materials

- hat and feather patterns on page 29
- 3 copies of the writing form on page 30
- 12" x 18" (30.5 x 45.5) blue construction paper for the hat
- red construction paper for the feather
- scissors and glue
- stapler

1 Cut the hat and feather from construction paper. Make three hat pieces and one feather.

2 Cut out each of the three writing forms. Glue one in each section of the hat.

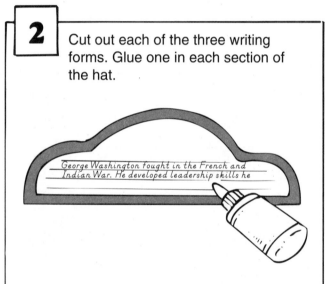

> George Washington fought in the French and Indian War. He developed leadership skills he

3 Staple the corners together. Glue the feather to one section.

Wear the "book" or display it on the bookcase with library books about this first president.

Writing Suggestions

Review George Washington's life. Write three important facts about George Washington. Tell why each fact influenced his success.

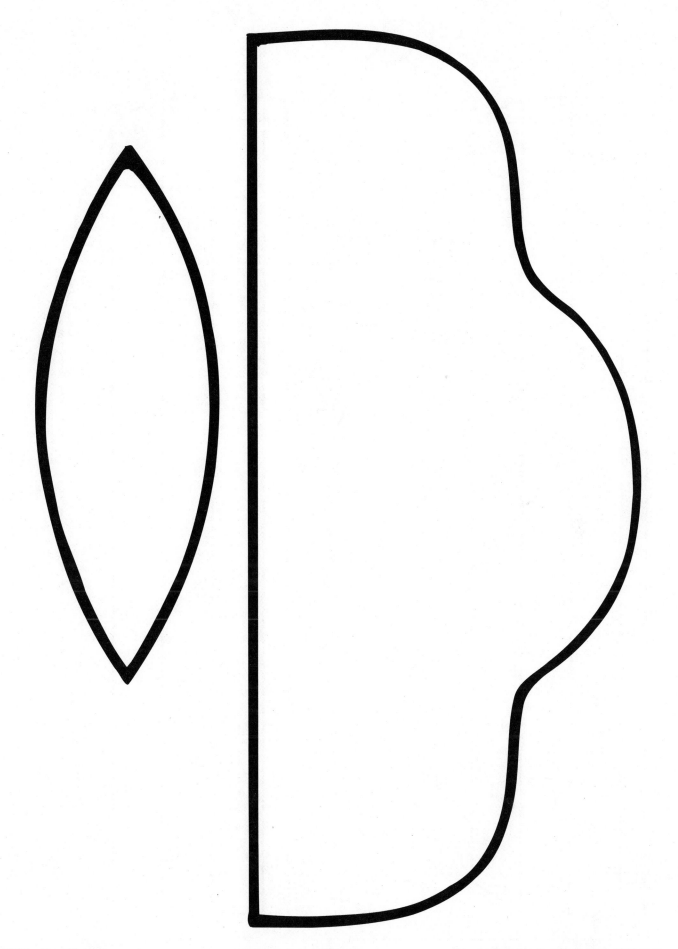

29

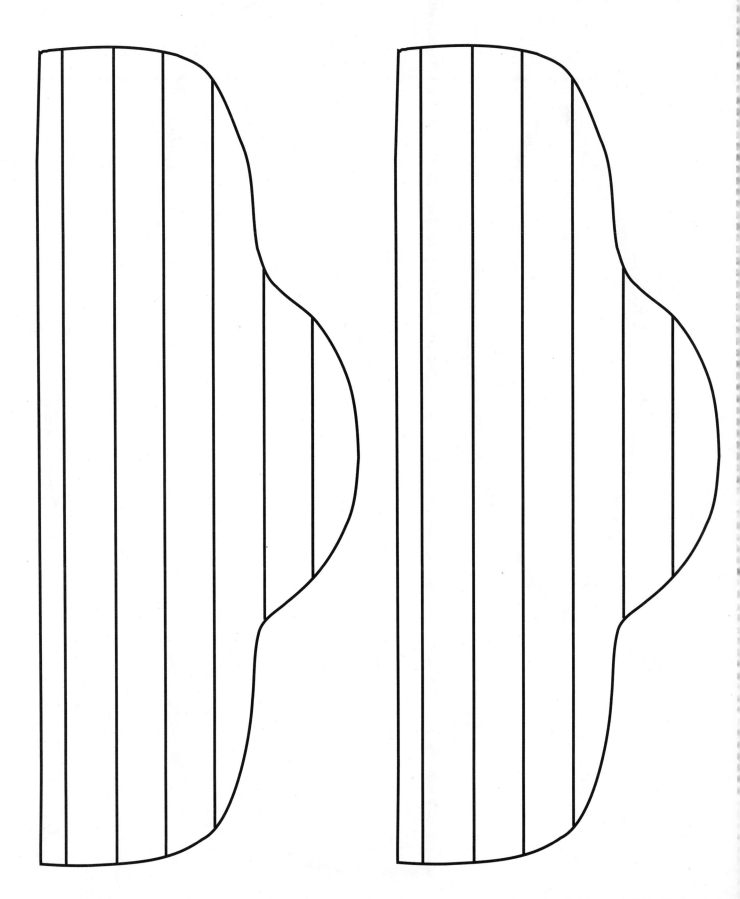

St. Patrick's Day

March 17

Background

St. Patrick's Day celebrates being of Irish descent. It is the feast day of St. Patrick, a Christian missionary to Ireland in the fifth century A.D. The celebration is noted for parades, wearin' o' the green, and good fellowship. It was first celebrated in the United States in 1737 in the city of Boston.

Books to Read

Clever Tom and the Leprechaun by Linda Shute; Scholastic, 1988.

The Hungry Leprechaun by Mary Calhoun; Morrow Junior Books, 1962.

Jamie O'Rourke and the Big Potato by Tomie de Paola; Putnam, 1992.

Jeremy Bean's St. Patrick's Day by Alice Schertle; Lothrop, Lee & Shepard, 1987.

The Luck of the Irish by Brendan Patrick Paulsen; Raintree Publishers, 1989.

Our St. Patrick's Day Book by Sandra Ziegler; Children's Press, 1987.

St. Patrick's Day in the Morning by Eve Bunting; Clarion Books, 1980.

Facts

- The symbol of St. Patrick's Day is the shamrock, a small three-leaved clover.

- The word *shamrock* comes from the Irish-Gaelic word "seamrog" meaning little clover.

- Thirty of the fifty states have St. Patrick's Day parades. The largest is in New York City where over 100,000 marchers parade up Fifth Avenue for six hours or more.

- Traditionally, magical little people called leprechauns join in the celebration. Any one who "catches" a leprechaun receives wishes and may learn where the leprechaun's pot of gold is hidden.

Leprechaun
An Individual Student Book

Materials

- 12" x 12" (30.5 x 30.5 cm) green construction paper
- leprechaun's head pattern on page 33
- writing form and shamrocks on page 34
- scissors, glue
- felt pens or crayons

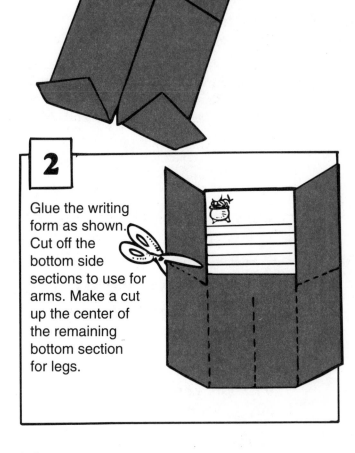

1

Fold the sides of green paper to the center.

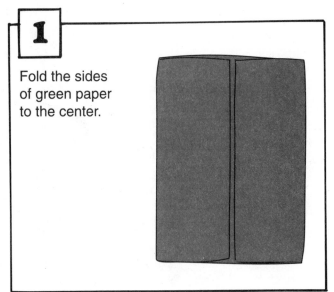

2

Glue the writing form as shown. Cut off the bottom side sections to use for arms. Make a cut up the center of the remaining bottom section for legs.

3

Color and cut out the head and shamrock patterns. Glue them to the body.

Writing Suggestions

Where does this leprechaun keep his pot of gold?

Why is the leprechaun smiling?

Does this leprechaun have a special secret?

Write an Irish tale to explain the answers.

33

How to Make Books with Children EMC 578

Easter

the first Sunday after the first full moon following the vernal equinox

Background

Easter is a time to celebrate new life. Christians celebrate the resurrection of Christ. The celebration began about the second century A.D. In America, Easter has become a day of church festivities, family gatherings, parades, and egg hunts. As the earth puts on its new greenery and spring flowers, people wear their new outfits and celebrate.

Books to Read

The April Rabbits by David Cleveland; Scholastic, 1978.

Bunny Trouble by Hans Wilhelm; Scholastic, 1985.

Chicken Sunday by Patricia Polacco; Philomel Books, 1992.

Little Rabbit's Easter Surprise by Kenn and Joanne Compton; Holiday House, 1992.

Max's Chocolate Chicken by Rosemary Wells; Dial Books for Young Readers, 1989.

Seven Eggs by Meredith Hooper; Harper & Row, 1985.

Today Is Easter by P. K. Hallinan; Forest House Publications, 1993.

Facts

- Since it represents rebirth, the egg became an Easter symbol.

- Easter egg hunts originated in Europe.

- Legend has it that the sun jumps for joy as it rises on Easter morning, so many services begin at sunrise.

- The tradition of coloring eggs probably began with medieval travelers to Egypt and Persia, where people colored eggs for their spring festivals.

Bunny's Surprise

A Class Book

Materials

- bunny pop-up pattern on page 37
- writing form on page 38
- 9" x 12" (23 x 30.5 cm) construction paper
- scissors, glue
- felt pens or crayons
- hole punch
- strip of rafia or ribbon

1 Color, cut, and fold the pop-up pattern.

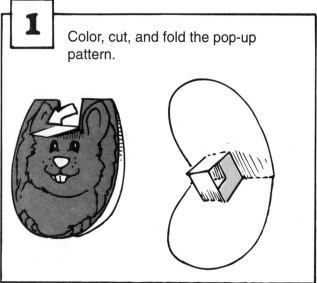

2 Glue the pop-up to the construction paper next to the writing form. Draw Bunny's surprise on the square. Glue it inside the pop-up.

3 Collect student stories together with a paper cover. Punch holes and bind with a strip of rafia or ribbon.

Writing Suggestions

Write a riddle to describe bunny's hidden surprise. Then lift the bunny to find the answer to the riddle.

Bunny's Surprise

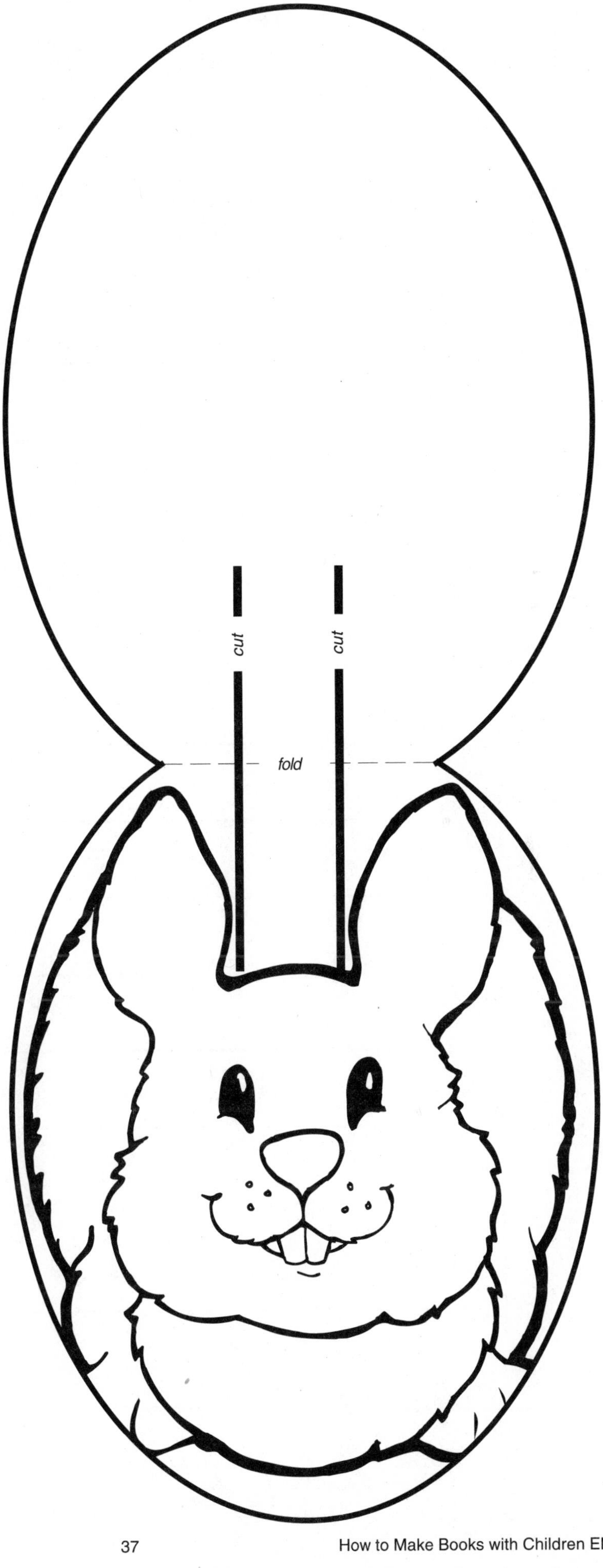

cut   cut

fold

How to Make Books with Children EMC 578

How to Make Books with Children EMC 578

April Fools' Day

April 1

Background

April Fools' Day is a day of tricks. Friends plan ways to make fools out of each other. It probably originated in France where a calendar change by King Charles IX moved the celebration of New Year's Day to January first. Those who celebrated the old day were called April Fools.

April Fools' Day is also the first day of National Humor Month. It's a great day for making someone laugh. It seems appropriate that April Fools' Day comes at a time when nature plays tricks on everyone, as it changes from showers to sunshine in an instant.

Books to Read

The April Fool by Alice Schertle; Lothrop, Lee & Shepard, 1981.

April Fool by Michelle Spirn; January Productions, 1983.

April Fools' Day Magic by James W. Baker; Lerner Publications, 1989.

Arthur's April Fool by Marc Brown; Little, Brown, 1983.

April Showers by George Shannon; Greenwillow Books, 1995.

It's April Fools' Day by Steven Kroll; Scholastic, 1990.

Look Out, It's April Fools' Day by Frank Modell; Greenwillow Books, 1985.

Facts

- In France children are given a chocolate fish on April 1. Early spring is the time that the young fish in the river are easier to catch than the older fish, so a silly or easily tricked person is called an April fish—*poisson d'avril*.

- The last day of the Hindu Festival of *Holie* on March 31 is like April Fools' Day. Unsuspecting persons are sent on fools' errands.

- Here's a joke for April Fools' Day:

  Person 1: What's long, green, and creepy with six legs and big teeth?

  Person 2: I don't know.

  Person 1: I don't know either, but there's one crawling up your leg.

April Fools to You

An Individual Student Book

Materials

- 9" x 12" (23 x 30.5 cm) construction paper
- pop-up writing form on page 41
- pop-up pattern on page 42
- scissors
- glue
- crayons or felt pens
- cover sheet on page 42

1 Fold the pop-up writing form.

2 Add the pop-up pattern to the form.

3 Fold the construction paper in half. Lay the folded pop-up in this folder. Put glue on the top of the pop-up. Close the folder. Flip it over and repeat on the other side.

Color the cover sheet and glue it to the front of the book.

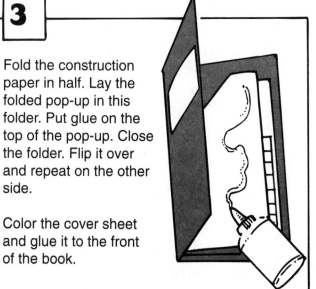

Writing Suggestions

Have you ever been tricked on April Fools' Day? How did you feel? What happened?

Write to explain your foolish moment.

How to Make Books with Children EMC 578

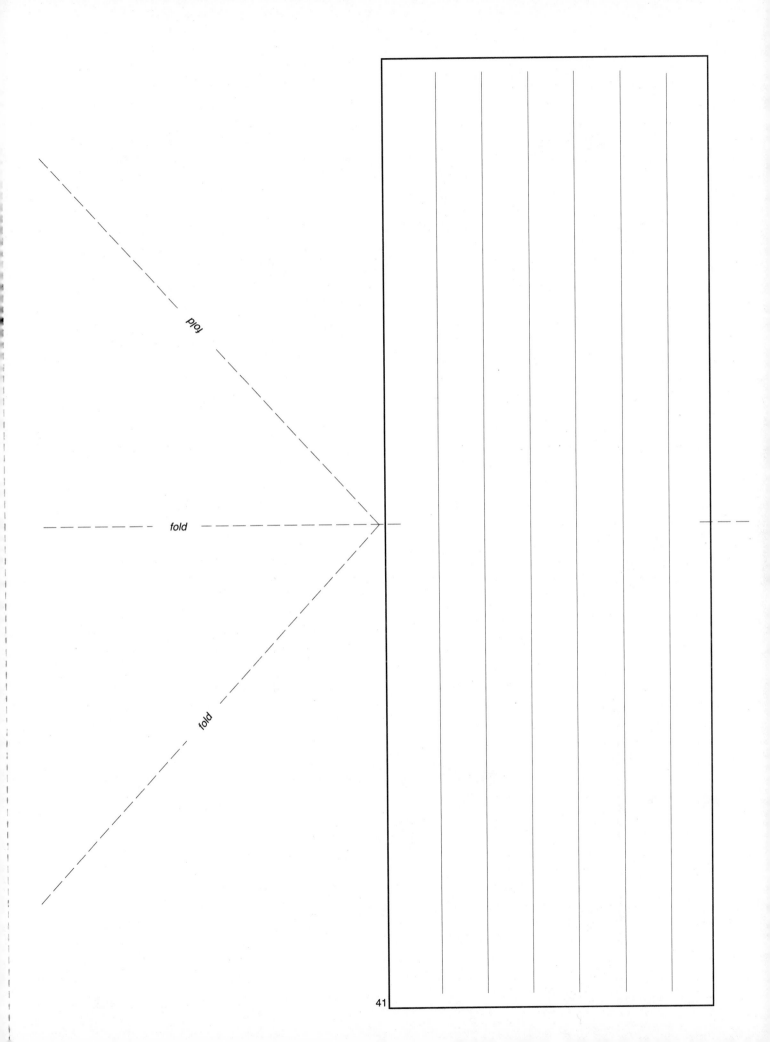

fold

fold

fold

41

April Fools' Day

by _____

How to Make Books with Children EMC 578

Songkran

April 13

Background

Songkran, the Water Festival, is celebrated in Thailand. It lasts for three days. Every-one celebrates by throwing water. It is the Thai way of blessing family and friends. People parade down the streets with enormous statues of Buddha, spraying water over the crowds. Everyone wades happily into ponds, canals, and rivers. They carry pans and buckets for scooping up the water. During the festival, children pour per-fumed water into their parents' hands as a sign of respect. Everywhere there is fun, laughter, and the sound of splashing water.

Books to Read

Splash by Susan Kovacs Buxbaum; Little, Brown, 1987.

Splish Splash by Joan Bransfield Graham; Ticknor & Fields, 1994.

The Trip of a Drip by Vicki Cobb; Little, Brown, 1986.

Water by Frank Asch; Harcourt Brace, 1995.

Water, Water Everywhere by Mark J. Rauzon and Cynthia Overbeck Bix; Sierra Club Books for Children, 1994.

The Wonder Thing by Libby Hathorn; Houghton Mifflin, 1996.

Facts

- On Songkran it is a blessing to be soaked, because the water washes away all the evils of the old year.

- Traditionally, Songkran is the day that the people of Thailand and Burma go to the temples to wash the statues of the Buddhas.

THAILAND

- To give animals new life, birds are released from their cages and fish are poured from their bowls into rivers.

The Big Splash

A Class Book

Materials

- 5" x 13 1/2" (13 x 31.5 cm) white construction paper
- pop-up form and patterns on page 46
- writing form on page 45
- 12" x 12" (30.5 x 30.5 cm) construction paper
- glue and scissors
- hole punch and two metal rings
- crayons or felt pens

1

4 1/2"

Fold the white paper. Glue the bucket on the lower section and have the child draw their face and body on the top section.

2

Cut and fold the pop-up. Glue the splash onto the tab. Glue the pop-up into the fold of the long white paper.

3

Assemble all student stories and add a paper cover. Add a title. Punch holes and use metal rings to bind all sheets together.

Glue the pop-up and writing form side-by-side on the large construction paper.

Writing Suggestions

Imagine that you threw a pot of water.
- Who will it splash?
- What will happen?
- How will you explain?

Write to tell about the *big splash*.

The Big Splash

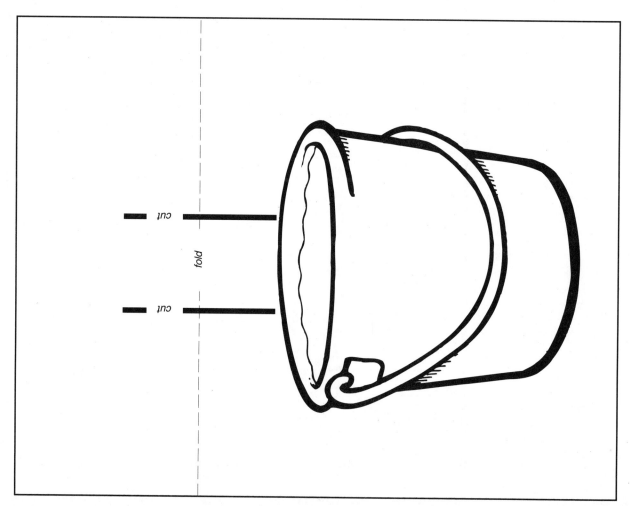

cut

fold

cut

Arbor Day

generally the last Friday in April

Background

Arbor Day is a day dedicated to trees. It was first celebrated in Nebraska on April 10, 1872 with the planting of over one million trees. The day is celebrated in different states on different days, but is usually near April 22, the birthday of Julius Sterling Morton, known as the "father of Arbor Day."

Books to Read

Arbor Day by Diane L. Burns; Carolrhoda Books, 1989.

Be a Friend to Trees by Patricia Lauber; HarperCollins, 1994.

Have You Seen Trees? by Joanne Oppenheim; Scholastic, 1995.

How Trees Help Me by Bobbie Kalman and Janine Schaub; Crabtree Publishing, 1992.

Its Arbor Day, Charlie Brown by Charles Schulz; Random House, 1977.

Once There Was a Tree by Natalia Aromanova; Dial Books, 1985.

Facts

- Arbor means *tree* in Latin.

- Julius Morton was editor of Nebraska's first newspaper. He had moved to the open prairie of Nebraska territory in 1854. He recognized Nebraska's need for trees and campaigned for a special day dedicated to planting them.

Mr. Morton wrote: "Other holidays repose upon the past—Arbor Day proposes for the future."

A Tree Home

A Class Book

Materials

- treetop form on page 49
- writing form on page 50
- 12" x 18" (30.5 x 45.5 cm) blue construction paper
- scissors
- crayons or felt pens
- hole punch
- 12" (30.5 cm) flexible twig

---

1 Cut out and fold the treetop pattern. Color the tree. Open the flaps and draw who is living in the tree.

2 Glue the treetop to the construction paper and draw the trunk. Glue the writing form next to the tree.

3 Place all student pages together and punch two holes in the left margin. Slip the twig through the holes to bind the pages together.

Writing Suggestions

Trees are homes to many different animals. Draw and write to show the animals that live in this tree. Tell how the tree provides their food and shelter.

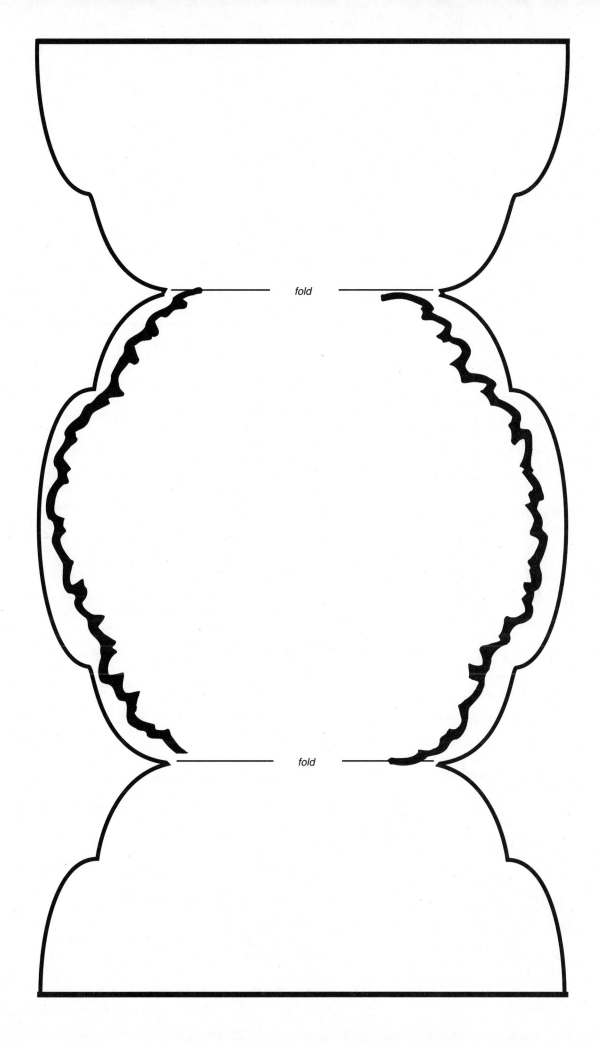

fold

fold

How to Make Books with Children EMC 578

Earth Day

April 22

Background

Set aside as a day to focus on taking care of the earth and its resources, the first Earth Day was held on April 22, 1970.

Books to Read

The Earth and I by Frank Asch; Harcourt Brace, 1994.

Earthdance by Joanne Ryder; Henry Holt & Co., 1996.

Every Day Is Earth Day by Illa Podendorf; Children's Press, 1971.

The Great Trash Bash by Loreen Leedy; Holiday House, 1991.

Just a Dream by Chris Van Ahlsburg; Houghton Mifflin, 1990.

The Kid's Earth Handbook by Sandra Markle; Atheneum, 1991.

The Lorax by Dr. Seuss; Random House, 1971.

The People Who Hugged Trees adapted by Deborah Lee Rose; Roberts Rinehart, 1990.

Save the Earth! An Ecology Handbook for Kids by Betty Miles; Knopf, 1974.

Tanya's Big Green Dream by Linda Glaser; Macmillan, 1994.

Facts

The Three Rs of Earth Day

Reduce = Cut down on garbage before you buy something.

Reuse = Save things that would usually be thrown out and use them over again.

Recycle = Reuse the materials that things are made of by using the materials in a new way.

used paper → pulp → new paper
glass bottles → crushed glass → new glass products

The Three Rs of Earth Day

An Individual Student Book

Materials

- globe pattern on page 53
- 3 copies of the writing form on page 54
- 1 paper shopping bag
- 2 paper fasteners
- hole punch and scissors
- crayons or felt pens

1 Color and cut out the globe. Glue it to the paper bag. Cut it out going through both layers of the bag. Leave a border. Now you have a front and back cover.

2 Fill in each of the writing forms. Use one form to explain each concept: reduce, reuse, and recycle.

3 Place the writing forms between the paper bag covers. Punch two holes on the left side and insert paper fasteners.

Writing Suggestions

Write ways that you can use the three Rs of Earth Day in your own life.

I can reduce...
I can reuse...
I can recycle...

53

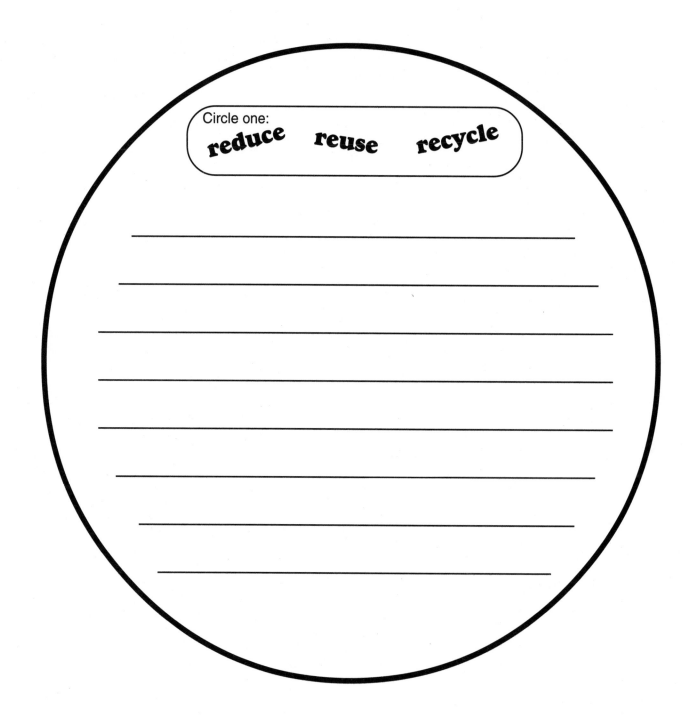

Circle one:

reduce   reuse   recycle

May Day

May 1

Background

May Day is celebrated as the day of passage between the seasons of winter and spring. It is one of the world's oldest holidays. It probably came from a Roman rite of spring when flower dances and processions were offered to Flora, the goddess of flowers. Flowers and fruit were given as gifts.

In modern celebrations May baskets are filled with flowers and hung on friends' doors. Dancers circle a flowering tree or Maypole as they "bring in the May."

Books to Read

The Flower Mother by Mary Calhoun; Morrow, 1972.

In the Spring by Craig Brown; Greenwillow Books, 1994.

Miss Flora McFlimsey's May Day by Mariana (Foster); Lothrop, Lee & Shepard, 1969.

My Spring Robin by Anne Rockwell; Macmillan, 1989.

We Celebrate Spring by Bobbie Kalman; Crabtree Publishing, 1985.

Facts

- The Maypole is usually a pine tree representing Attis, the god of vegetation.

- In old England it was believed that you could make freckles disappear if you faced east and washed your face with dew before dawn on the first of May.

- People gather flowers and tree branches to decorate their homes to "bring in the May."

A May Wish Basket

An Individual Student Book

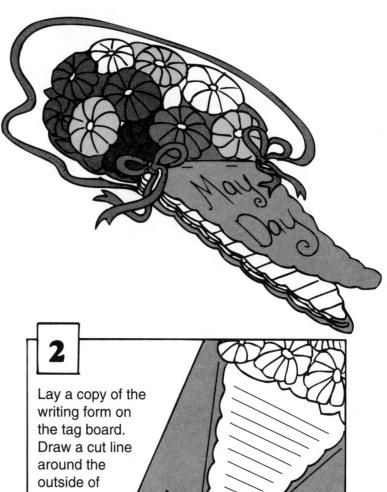

Materials

- writing form on page 57
- bouquet pattern on page 58
- 12" x 18" (30.5 x 45.5 cm) tag board
- 9" x 12" (23 x 30.5 cm) construction paper
- 25" (64 cm) piece of yarn or ribbon
- 2 paper fasteners
- glue
- hole punch, scissors
- crayons or felt pens

1 Color the bouquet pattern. Glue the cut out pattern to the tag board.

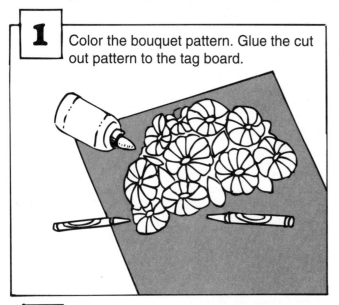

2 Lay a copy of the writing form on the tag board. Draw a cut line around the outside of the bouquet and form. Cut it out.

3 Cut a front cover from construction paper the same size as the writing form. Lay the forms and the cover on the bouquet. Punch 4 holes. Insert 2 paper fasteners through the inside holes and tie the yarn through the outside ones.

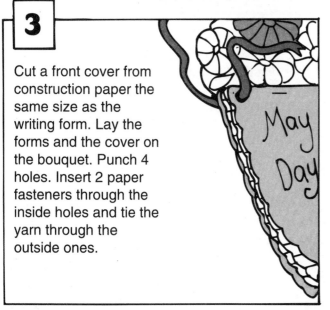

Writing Suggestions

Write a wish to go with your May Basket.

Hang the basket on the door of a friend and ring the doorbell. Then run and hide.

Watch to see if the flower basket and the wish make your friend smile.

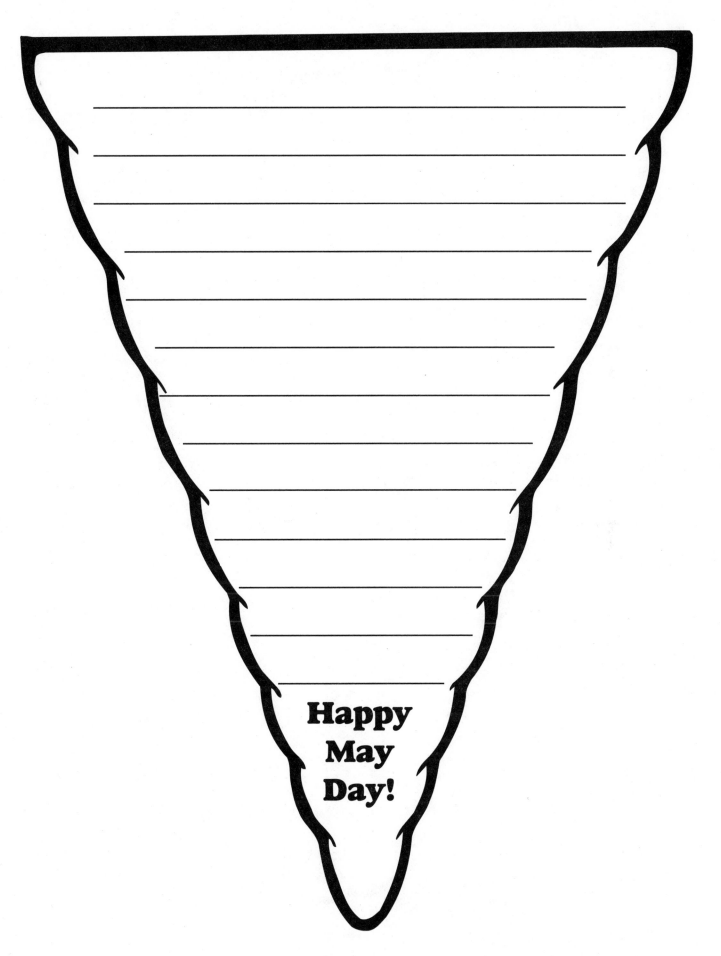

Happy May Day!

How to Make Books with Children EMC 578

Mother's Day

the second Sunday in May

Background

The idea for Mother's Day began centuries ago when Romans paid tribute to mothers at a spring festival called Hilaria. Much later, young men and women in England returned home on Mothering Sunday to honor their mothers with gifts and a special mothering cake. In the United States, President Wilson officially proclaimed the first Mother's Day in 1914.

Books to Read

All in a Day's Work by Louise Mandrell and Ace Collins; The Summit Group, 1993.

Happy Mother's Day by Steven Kroll; Holiday House, 1985.

Hooray for Mother's Day! by Marjorie Weinman Sharmat; Holiday House, 1986.

The Mother's Day Mice by Eve Bunting; Clarion Books, 1986.

The Mother's Day Sandwich by Jillian Wynot; Orchard Books, 1990.

Mother's Mother's Day by Lorna Balian; Abingdon, 1982.

Facts

- Miss Anna Jarvis from Philadelphia was instrumental in the campaign for Mother's Day. She never married and was never a mother. She chose the carnation as the symbol of motherly love because her mother loved carnations.

- The special mothering cakes of old England were rich fruit cakes that were boiled and then baked.

- In Africa, Mother's Day is celebrated on the first Sunday in May. In Argentina mothers are honored in October, and in Norway the celebration is in February.

Mother's Many Faces
A Class Book

Materials

- the frame pattern on page 61
- the writing form on page 62
- 5" x 12" (13 x 30.5 cm) strip of white construction paper
- 12" x 18" (30.5 x 45.5 cm) piece of colored construction paper
- scissors, glue, mat knife
- felt pens or crayons
- hole punch and ribbon

 1

Color and cut out the frame. Cut the slits in the picture frame with a mat knife.

Slip the white paper through the cut lines and draw Mother. Pull the strip further and draw her again. Repeat. Now you have three pictures of her.

2

Glue the frame and the writing form to the large construction paper.

3

Bind all student stories together by punching holes and tying a bow through each hole.

Writing Suggestions

Mothers wear different faces at different times. Describe and draw these faces and then write about them.

- Mom at her job
- Mom at a picnic
- Mom at breakfast
- Mom at my bedtime

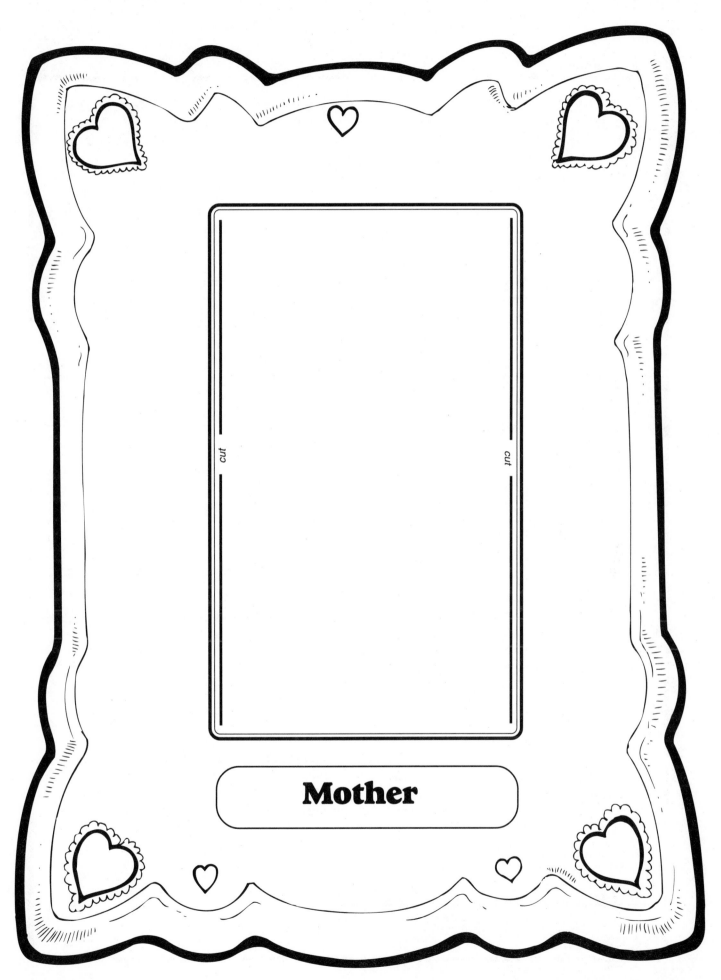

cut

cut

Mother

How to Make Books with Children EMC 578

My Mother

How to Make Books with Children EMC 578

Kodomo-No-Hi

May 5

Background

Kodomo-No-Hi is a day when Japanese families honor their children. It is sometimes called the Feast of Flags. Originally it was a day for honoring only sons. One flag was flown for each boy in the family. The flags, made in the shape of carp, flew from the roof or a tall pole set up in the garden. Carp are strong fish that swim up fast-moving streams. To the Japanese, they symbolize courage.

Today Japanese families recognize each of their children with a fish flag and wish for courage to last throughout their lives.

Books to Read

A Carp for Kimiko by Virginia L. Kroll; Charlesbridge, 1993.

Japan by Karen Jacobsen; Children's Press, 1982.

Japan by Sheila Dalton; Grolier, 1989.

Facts

- Boys and girls go to Shinto shrines where priests wave white paper streamers over their heads, bless them, and wish them health and happiness.

- The flag or kite for the oldest child is flown at the top of the pole and is the largest one. It might be fifteen feet long.

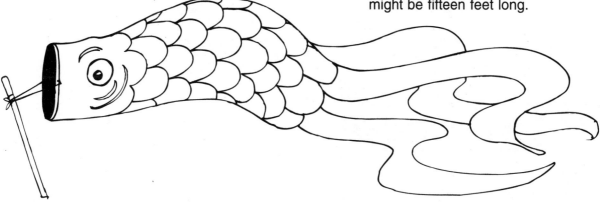

How to Make Books with Children EMC 578

Fish Kites

An Individual Student Book

Materials _____

- fish pattern on page 65
- writing form on page 66
- 2 sheets of 9" x 12" (23 x 30.5 cm) construction paper
- paper scraps
- 1" x 8" (2.5 x 20 cm) tissue paper or cloth strips
- 2 paper fasteners, paper clip, and hole punch
- glue, scissors
- felt pens

1

Color the fish pattern with bright colors.
Cut it out. Glue it to the construction paper. Clip the two pieces of construction together and cut out the shape.

2

Cut a fin from paper scraps. Write the student's name on the fin and glue it to the fish. Glue on the strips for the tail.

3

Put the writing form between the two covers and bind it all together by punching two holes and inserting the paper fasteners.

Writing Suggestions _____

Write about the ways in which you are strong and persistent like the carp.

How to Make Books with Children EMC 578

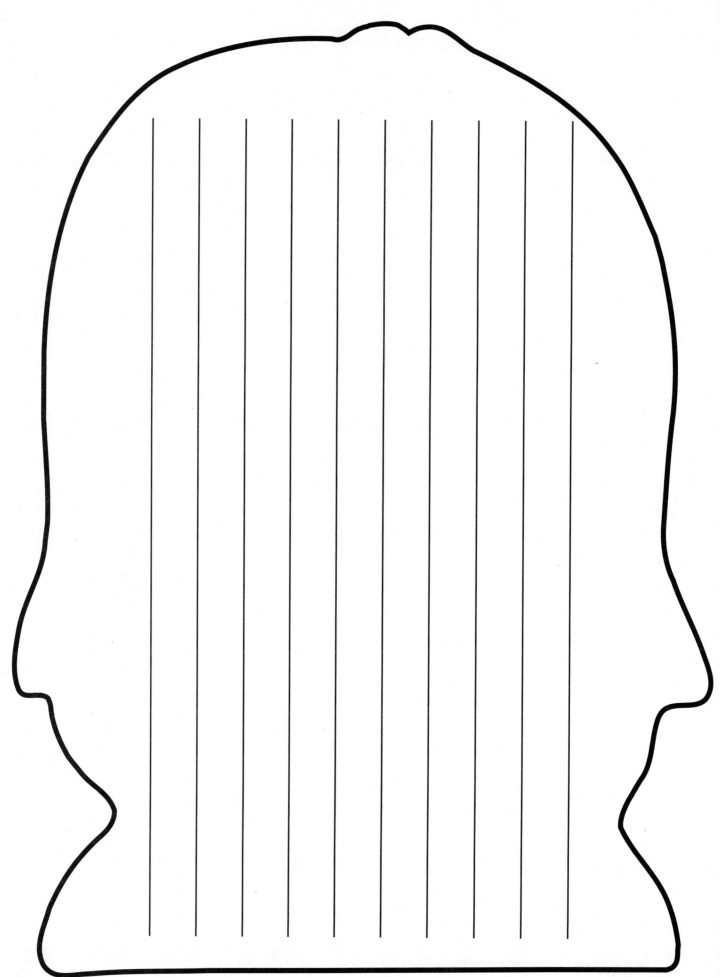

How to Make Books with Children EMC 578

Cinco de Mayo

May 5

Background

Cinco de Mayo is an important political holiday in Mexico. It commemorates the day that Benito Juarez lead his followers to victory when the French invaded Mexico in 1862. He carried on the struggle until the French-imposed empire of Maximilian fell in 1867.

Juarez was born to Zapotec Indian parents who died when he was three. He spoke only his native Zapotec language and received no education until he was twelve. He went to Oaxaca City and learned Spanish and was educated by a Franciscan monk. Eventually he studied law and became the champion of Mexican liberalism.

The celebration of Cinco de Mayo includes grand parades, mock battles, dances, fireworks, and flower festivals.

Books to Read

Cinco de Mayo by Maria Viramontes de Marin; Marin Publications, 1990.

Fiesta! Cinco de Mayo by June Behrens; Children's Press, 1978.

Fiesta! Mexico's Great Celebrations by Elizabeth Silverthorne; Millbrook Press, 1992.

Facts

Mexican Fiestas often include the breaking of piñatas. The piñata, a clay pot decorated and filled with treats, is strung up overhead. Children take turns being blindfolded and poking at the piñata with a long stick. When the piñata is broken, the goodies inside tumble to the ground for all to share.

Yo no quiero oro, ni quiero plata.
   (Yo no kee-AIR-o O-ro, nee kee-AIR-o PLAH-ta)

!Yo lo que quiero es quebrar la pinata!
   (Yo lo kay kee-AIR-o es kay-BRAR la pee-NYA-ta!)

Gold and silver do not matter.
All I want is to break the pinata!

The Piñata

An Individual Student Book

The Piñata

Materials

- pop-up pattern on page 69
- additional patterns on page 70
- 9" x 12" (23 x 30.5 cm) construction paper
- 5" (13 cm) piece of paper drinking straw
- scissors, mat knife and glue
- felt pens or crayons

1 Cut and fold the pop-up pattern.

2 Color and cut out the child. Cut the marked slits with a mat knife and slip the straw through. Glue child to the pop-up tab.

Draw a piñata on the other pattern. Fold down the flap and glue it to the top of the paper.

3 Fold the construction paper in half. Glue the pop-up into the fold. (See page 3) Close the book and glue on the title and author's name.

Writing Suggestions

Write about Mexican Fiestas.

Tell what amazing thing came out of the piñata.

Try writing a new piñata chant.

glue here

The Piñata

fold

cut

cut

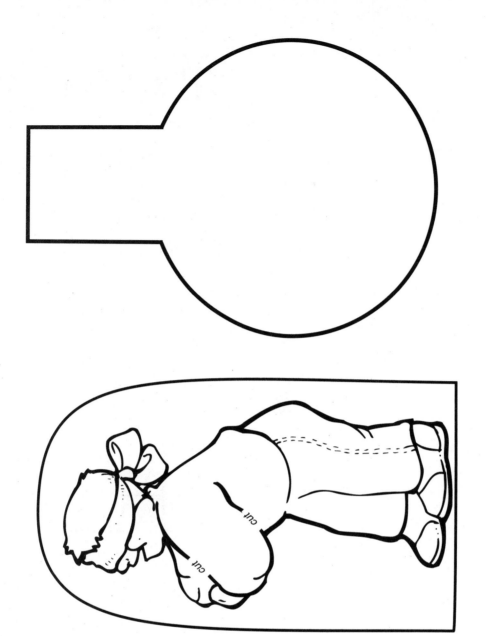

The Piñata

by _____

How to Make Books with Children EMC 578

Flag Day

June 14

Background

The first American flag had seven red and six white stripes with thirteen white stars upon a blue background. It became the official U.S. flag on June 14, 1777. The first official Flag Day was held in Philadelphia in 1893. It is a day of flying flags, parading, and patriotic speeches.

Books to Read

The American Flag by Ann Armbruster; Franklin Watts, 1991.

The Flag We Love by Pam Munoz Ryan; Charlesbridge, 1996.

A New Flag for a New Country by June Behrens; Children's Press, 1975.

Our Flag by Eleanor Ayer; Millbrook Press, 1992.

Saga of the American Flag by Candice M. DeBarr; Harbinger House, 1990.

Facts

- Francis Scott Key wrote the famous words of **The Star Spangled Banner** as he watched the bombing of Ft. McHenry during the War of 1812 (September 1814). The Ft. McHenry flag had 15 stars and 15 stripes. The flag is on display in the Smithsonian Institution in Washington, D.C.

- The New Flag Act of 1818, sponsored by Peter W. Wendover from New York City, set the permanent number of stripes on the flag at 13 and provided that the number of stars match the number of states.

- Today's U.S. flag has gone through 66 variations.

The American Flag

A Class Book

Materials

- flag pattern on page 73, writing form on page 74
- 12" x 18" (30.5 x 45.5 cm) sheet of red construction paper
- blue tempera paint, white tempera paint
- pencil with eraser
- scissors, glue
- crayons or felt pens
- hole punch
- 20" (51 cm) of red yarn
- 3 paper fasteners

1 Color the red stripes on the flag. Paint the field blue. Allow to dry. Stamp "stars" by dipping the eraser end of a pencil in white paint.

Star pattern is a row of 6 stars alternating with a row of 5 stars, for a total of 9 rows.

2 Glue the flag pattern and the writing form on the construction paper.

3 Add a construction paper cover. Bind all students stories together by punching two holes along the **top** margin.

Insert paper fasteners and yarn to provide a hanger for the book. Tear strips of white paper to paste on cover. Add some gold stars, and title.

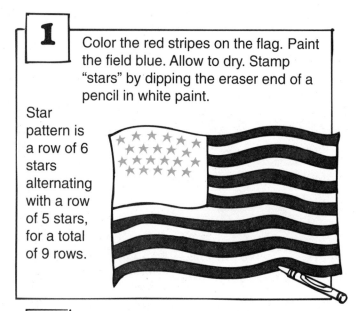

Writing Suggestions

Write about what the flag means to you.

What can you do to show respect to the flag?

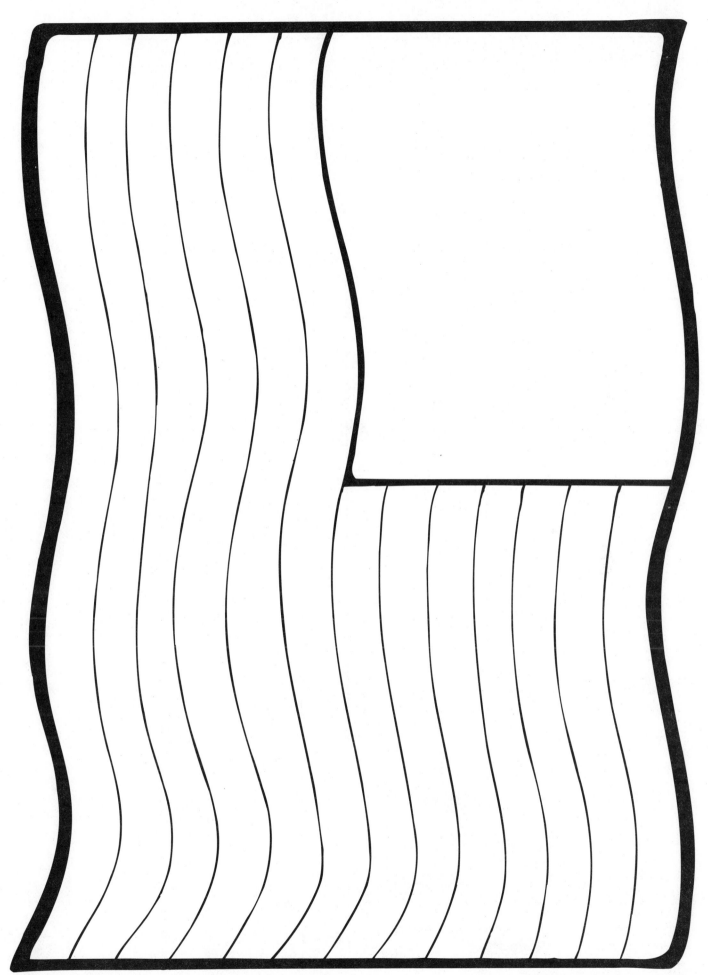

73

Name

Flag Day

June 14

How to Make Books with Children EMC 578

Father's Day

the third Sunday in June

Background

The celebration of a Father's Day can be traced to the ancient Romans who honored their departed parents between February 13 and 22. However, Father's Day is one of our newest holidays. It wasn't until 1972 that President Richard Nixon signed a congressional resolution assigning an official day of honor to fathers.

Books to Read

Always My Dad by Dennis Wyeth; Apple Soup Books, 1995.

I Love My Dad Because... by Laurel Porter-Gaylord;   Dutton Children's Books, 1991.

Just Me and Dad by Mercer Mayer; Western Publishing, 1977.

My Dad is Awesome by Nick Butterworth; Candlewick Press, 1992.

My Daddy the Magnificent by Kristy Parker; Dutton Children's Books, 1987.

My Dad's a Wizard by Hannah Roche and Chris Fisher; De Agostini Editions, 1996.

A Perfect Father's Day by Eve Bunting; Clarion Books, 1991.

Facts

- Harry C. Meek, spokesman for the Lion's Clubs, is known as the originator of Father's Day.

- Willie Smart was a Civil War Veteran whose wife died in childbirth. He successfully brought up a daughter and five sons. In 1909 his daughter, Louise Smart Dodd, proposed a holiday honoring fathers. This was the first Father's Day celebration.

My Dad

A Class Book

Materials

- 6" x 18" (15 x 45.5 cm) white construction paper
- writing form on page 77
- paper scraps in assorted colors
- 9" x 12" (23 x 30.5 cm) colored construction paper
- scissors and glue
- hole punch and one metal ring
- crayons or felt pens

1

Fold the white paper in half to make the shirt shape. Measure 1 1/4" (3 cm) down from the fold. On each side cut 1 1/4" (3 cm) toward the center. Fold the flaps down and inward to form the collar. Color it to look like one your Dad might wear.

2

Glue the writing form inside the shirt. Glue the shirt to the colored construction paper. Write the father's name in the name block and glue it below the shirt.

3

Bind all student's stories together by punching a hole in the upper left corner and inserting a metal ring.
Design a cover. Let each student be listed as an author.

Writing Suggestions

1. Make a list of the things that your dad does.
2. Use the list to write a story about your dad.

The important thing about my dad is he fixes things.
He goes to work.
He plays golf.
He shaves every morning.
He gives great hugs.
But the important thing about my dad is he fixes things.

How to Make Books with Children EMC 578

Things my dad does:

My father's full name is:

_____

- -

_____

Independence Day

July 4

Background

The Fourth of July is the greatest patriotic holiday in the United States. It is the anniversary of the signing of the Declaration of Independence by the Continental Congress in 1776. July Fourth celebrations include fireworks, military reviews, barbecues, parades, flying of flags, and patriotic speeches.

Books to Read

America's Birthday by Tom Shachtman; Macmillan, 1986.

Celebrating Independence Day by Sally Nielsen; Abdo, 1992.

Fireworks, Picnics, and Flags by James Cross Giblin; Clarion Books, 1983.

Fourth of July by Lynda Sorensen; The Rourke Press, 1994.

The Glorious Fourth at Prairietown by Joan Anderson; Morrow, 1986.

Henrietta's Fourth of July by Syd Hoff; Garrard Publishing, 1981.

Hurray for the Fourth of July by Wendy Watson; Clarion Books, 1992.

My First Fourth of July Book by Harriet W. Hodgson; Children's Press, 1987.

Facts

- Bells were rung to celebrate the first public reading of the final draft of the Declaration of Independence in Philadelphia in 1776. Today many U.S. towns and cities continue this tradition by ringing bells on the Fourth of July.

- The first observance of Independence Day was in Philadelphia, Pennsylvania, 1877.

- Three former United States Presidents have died on July 4. Thomas Jefferson and John Adams both died on July 4, 1826. James Monroe died on July 4, 1831.

Fireworks

A Class Book

Materials

- a rocket pattern on page 80
- writing form on page 81
- 3" x 18" (7.5 x 45.5 cm) strip of dark blue construction paper
- 9" x 12" (23 x 30.5 cm) red construction paper
- 4" x 12" (x 30.5 cm) paper strip or cloth
- white and yellow tempera paint
- yellow pencils with erasers
- scissors, glue
- stapler

1

Accordion fold the blue paper in thirds. Cut out the rocket and glue it to the first panel.

Use tempera paint printed with the pencil eraser to create the rocket's fiery trail.

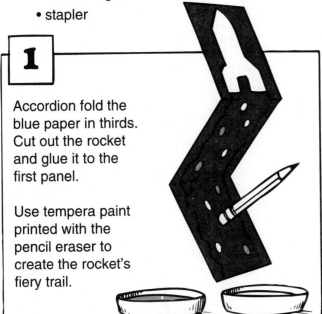

2

Glue the folded rocket and the writing form to the construction paper.

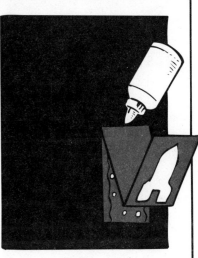

3

Staple student essays together and cover the staples with a paper flap or cloth tape. Decorate the cover with the star patterns provided.

Writing Suggestions

Think of the ways that you are proud to be an American. Write an essay explaining why you are proud of your country.

How to Make Books with Children EMC 578

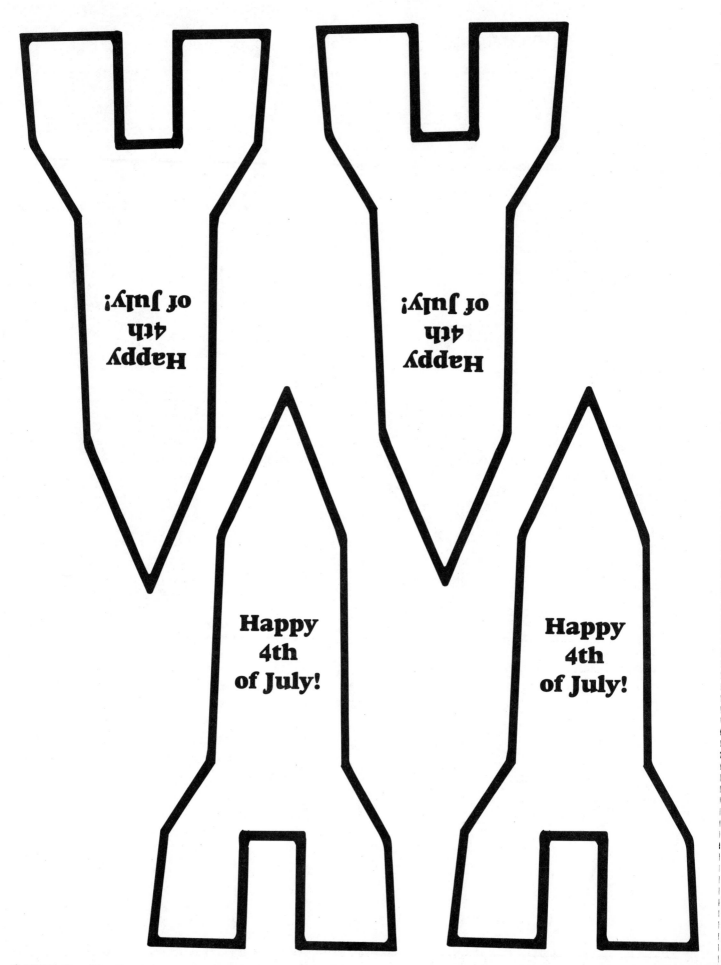

Happy
4th
of July!

Happy
4th
of July!

Independence Day

by_____

How to Make Books with Children EMC 578

National Aviation Day

August 19

Background

National Aviation Day is a celebration of America's progress in aviation. The first Aviation Day was held in 1939. August nineteenth was chosen because Orville Wright was born on August 19, 1871. Orville and his brother, Wilbur, built an "aeroplane" they called the *Flyer*. It had double wings. propellers and a small gasoline-powered engine. On December 17, 1903, at Kitty Hawk, North Carolina, Orville and the *Flyer* flew. It was the first time a manned machine was airborne through its own power.

Books to Read

Flight edited by Donald Lopez; Nature Company Discoveries Libraries, 1995.

The Glorious Flight by Alice Provensen; Viking Press, 1983.

Take Me Out to the Airfield! by Robert Quackenbush; Parents' Magazine Press, 1976.

Up in the Air by Myra Cohn Livingston; Holiday House, 1989.

The Wright Brothers by Russell Freedman; Holiday House, 1991.

Young Orville and Wilbur Wright; First to Fly by Andrew Woods; Troll Associates, 1992.

Facts

- The Wright brothers' first flight lasted twelve seconds.

- Wilbur, 36, and Orville, 32, ran a small bicycle company. They built scale models and full-size gliders as a hobby.

- In the 1920s and 30s the first passenger airplanes appeared in the United States. Airports consisted of passenger terminals and grass landing fields.

- German Heinkel He-178 was the first jet to fly. It first took off in August 1939.

- In 1947, American Chuck Yeager broke the "sound barrier" in his rocket plane. Until then, many people had thought that the destructive shockwaves of high speed flight were impossible to overcome.

Famous Airplanes

A Class Book

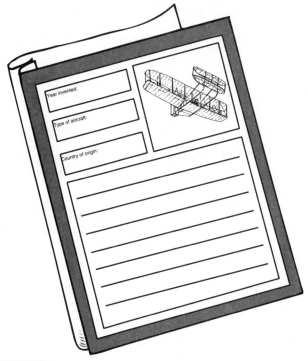

Materials

- report form on page 85
- airplane clipart on pages 84
- 9" x 12" (23 x 30.5 cm) construction paper for covers
- scissors and glue
- paper fasteners and hole punch
- magazines

1 Let students choose the airplane they wish to learn more about. They may use one of the clipart pictures or draw their own.

2 Put the reports in the order in which they appeared in history.

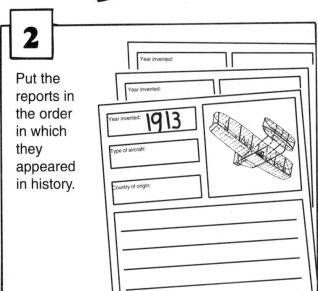

3 Bind the reports together inside a construction paper cover. Create a collage look by tearing "sky and cloud" pictures from magazines and pasting them in an overlapping manner.

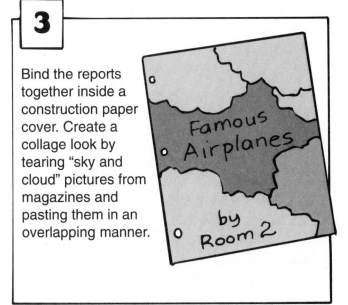

Writing Suggestions

Students can follow the outline presented on the writing form to write simple reports about aircraft.

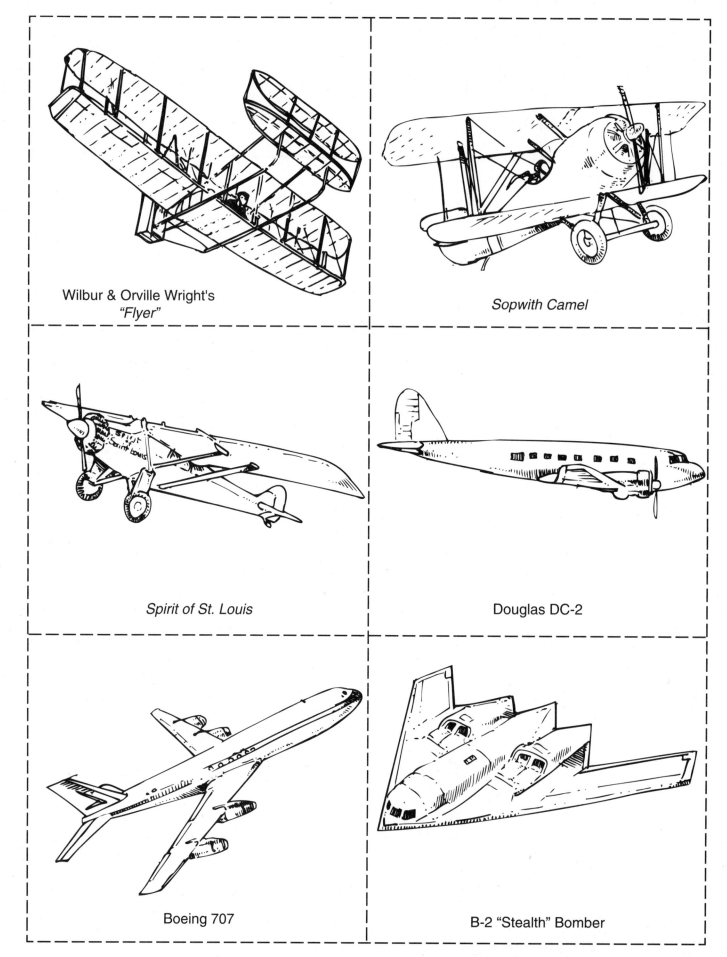

Wilbur & Orville Wright's
"Flyer"

Sopwith Camel

Spirit of St. Louis

Douglas DC-2

Boeing 707

B-2 "Stealth" Bomber

Name of aircraft:

Year invented:

Country of origin:

Describe the aircraft's features, history, and use:

Reported by:

Grandparents' Day
the first Sunday after Labor Day

Background

Grandparents' Day is observed nationally on the first Sunday after Labor Day. The purpose of the day is to visit grandparents or elderly shut-ins, giving them recognition and showing appreciation of them.

Books to Read

Gramma's Walk by Anna Grossnickle Hines; Greenwillow Books, 1993.

Grandaddy's Place by Helen V. Griffith; Greenwillow Books, 1987.

Grandfather by Jeannie Baker; Andre Deutsch, 1977.

Grandpa's Garden Lunch by Judith Casely; Greenwillow Books, 1990.

Grandpa's Slide Show by Deborah Gould; Lothrop, Lee & Shepard, 1987.

Happy Birthday, Grampie by Susan Pearson; Dial Books for Young Readers, 1987.

Journey by Patricia MacLachlan; Delacorte Press, 1991.

Our Granny by Margaret Wild; Ticknor & Fields, 1994.

Poppy's Chair by Karen Hesse; Macmillan, 1993.

A Window of Time by Audrey O. Leighton; Nadja Publishers, 1995.

Our Grandparents
A Class Book

Materials

- writing form on page 88
- 5" x 7" (13 x 18 cm) white construction paper
- 9" x 12" (23 x 30.5 cm) sheets construction paper for covers
- crayons or felt pens
- hole punch
- glue
- yarn

1 Students draw a picture of their grandparents on the white paper.

2 Put glue on the top strip of the writing form and attach the picture.

3 Put all the writing forms together and place between construction paper covers. Punch holes down the left margin and bind with the yarn.

Writing Suggestions

Write a list of rules for being a grandparent. You may want to give specific examples of things that your grandparents do.

Rules for Being a Grandparent

1. A grandparent must always have a cookie jar filled with ginger snaps.
2. A grandparent must know where the worms are hiding in the garden.
3. A grandparent must tell great stories and be a good hugger.

My Grandparents

glue

Their names:

_____

_____

Citizenship Day

September 17

Background

Citizenship Day is celebrated each year on September 17, the date on which the U.S. Constitution was signed in 1787. Many states hold ceremonies admitting new citizens to the U.S. on this day.

The current holiday was established in 1952. It is a combination of Constitution Day and I Am an American Day. Constitution Day was first observed in 1887 to honor the constitution's anniversary. I Am an American Day, originally celebrated in May, honored naturalized citizens.

Books to Read

Citizenship by Jay Schleiger; Rosen Publication Group, 1990.

How Many Days to America? by Eve Bunting; Clarion Books, 1988.

How to Become a United States Citizen: A Step-By-Step Guidebook by Sally Abel Schreuder; Nolo Press, 1983.

I Was Dreaming to Come to America— Memories from the Ellis Island Oral History Project selected by Veronica Lawlor; Viking Press, 1995.

A Very Important Day by Maggie Rugg Herold; Morrow Junior Books, 1995.

Oath of a New Citizen

I hereby declare, on oath, that I absolutely and entirely renounce and abjure all allegiance and fidelity to any foreign prince, potentate, state, or sovereignty of whom or which I have heretofore been a subject or citizen; that I will support and defend the Constitution and laws of the United States of America against all enemies, foreign and domestic; that I will bear true faith and allegiance to the same; that I will bear arms on behalf of the United States when required by the law; that I will perform noncombatant service in the Armed Forces of the United States when required by law; that I will perform work of national importance under civilian direction when required by the law; and that I take this obligation freely without any mental reservation or purpose of evasion, so help me God.

Statue of Liberty
A Class Book

Materials

- Statue of Liberty form on page 91
- writing form on page 91
- a copy of the *Oath of a New Citizen* on page 89*
- 9" x 12" (23 x 30.5 cm) red and blue construction paper
- scissors and glue
- hole punch and strips of string
- 8 1/2" x 9" (21.5 x 23 cm) construction paper for cover
- small flags

1 Fold back 3 1/2" (9 cm) on the long side of the construction paper. Glue the Statue of Liberty pattern on the flap.

2 Glue the writing form and Citizenship Oath on the inside section.

3 Use the smaller paper as a cover. Punch holes in the left margin of student papers and fasten with string pieces. Decorate cover.

Writing Suggestions

Think about what it means to be a citizen of the United States. Write about your feelings.

* This oath contains complex language. Explain unfamiliar words and concepts and guide students to explain the oath in their own words.

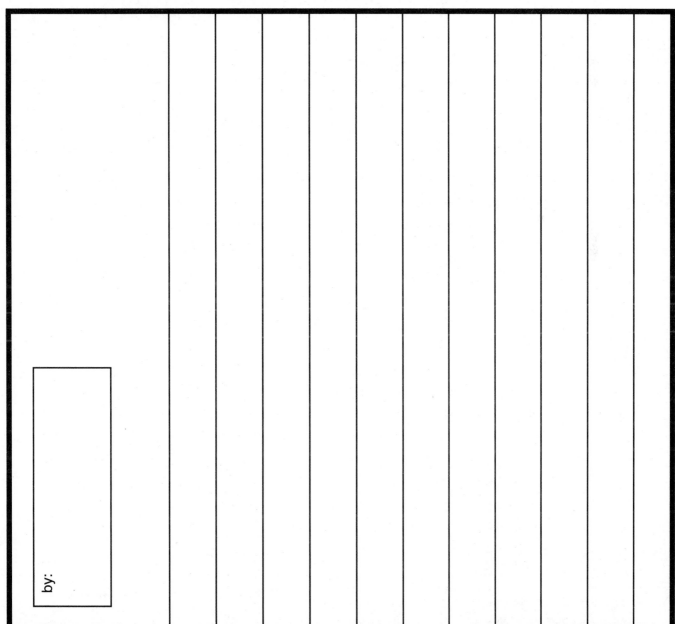

by:

Native American Day

the fourth Friday in September

Background

Native American Day is a day dedicated to recognizing and honoring Native Americans and their cultures. Native Americans have lived in this hemisphere for thousands of years. Their gifts to later settlers include maize, popcorn, squash, peanuts, dances, arts and crafts, and many words and names. Over half of the U.S. states have Native American names as well as hundreds of towns, rivers, lakes, and mountains.

Originally called American Indian Day, it was first observed in New York in 1912 under the direction of Dr. Arthur C. Parker who suggested the idea to the Boy Scouts.

Books to Read

Ceremony—In the Circle of Life by White Deer of Autumn; Raintree Publishers, 1983.

Drumbeat...Heartbeat by Susan Braine; Lerner Publications, 1995.

Eagle Drum on the Powwow Trail with a Young Grass Dancer by Robert Crum; Four Winds Press, 1994.

The Ledgerbook of Thomas Blue Eagle by Jewel H. Grutman and Gay Matthaei; Thomasson-Grant, 1994.

Powwow by George Ancona; Harcourt Brace Jovanovich, 1993.

Powwow by June Behrens; Children's Press, 1983.

Facts

- When Columbus sighted the New World in 1492 there were 1,100,000 Native Americans living on the land North of Mexico.

- In 1900 war and disease had reduced this number to 250,000.

- Between 1880 and 1920 the American government attempted to change the Indian way of life: Indian children were sent to boarding or day schools, Indian men were told to cut their hair, tribal dances were made illegal.

- In 1924, the U.S. officially recognized the rights of Indians as individual citizens and gave them the right to vote.

- In 1970, there were 669,000 Native Americans living in North America.

Parfleche *

An Individual Student Book

Materials

- 12" x 18" (30.5 x 45.5 cm) strip of brown paper bag
- writing form on page 94
- 4 paper fasteners
- yarn pieces
- scissors
- felt pens or crayons

1 Fold down 2" (5 cm) on the long side of the paper bag. Glue the writing form in the center of the parfleche. Fold up a flap on the bottom.

2 Fold side flaps around edges of the writing form, approximately 5" (13 cm) on each side. Decorate the flaps.

3 Fold up the *parfleche* and insert two paper fasteners through the flaps as shown. Tie yarn strips to the fasteners.

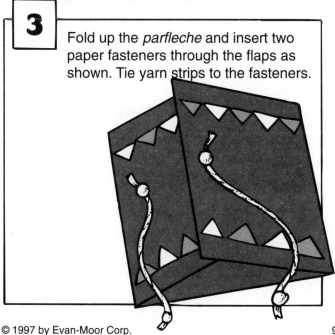

Writing Suggestions

Honor Native Americans by remembering the gifts that they gave to the development of the United States and the contributions that they continue to make. Write a thank you note in honor of Native American Day.

* The parfleche, generally made from buffalo hide, was the plains Indians' tote bag. It carried personal belongings, clothing, or food when these nomadic people were on the move following the buffalo herds.

Native American Day

by:

Columbus Day

October 12

Background

This holiday is the anniversary of the day Christopher Columbus landed in the Western Hemisphere in 1492. He had set sail from Palos, Spain, on August 3, 1492, with three ships: the Niña, Pinta, and Santa Maria. He finally reached America (Watling Island in the Bahamas) on October 12. Columbus thought that he had arrived in India.

In 1937 President Franklin D. Roosevelt signed a proclamation designating October 12 as a national holiday.

Books to Read

The Admiral and the Deck Boy by Genevieve O'Connor; Shoe Tree Press, 1991.

A Book About Christopher Columbus by Ruth Belov Gross; Scholastic, 1994.

Follow the Dream by Peter Sis; Knopf, 1991.

I, Christopher Columbus by Lisl Weil; Atheneum, 1983.

The Log of Christopher Columbus by Christopher Columbus; Philomel Books, 1992.

Pedro's Journal by Pam Conrad; Caroline Houses, 1991.

A Picture Book of Christopher Columbus by David A. Adler; Holiday House, 1991.

Facts

• Christopher Columbus was born in 1453.

• As a child Columbus went with his father, a weaver and wine merchant, on trading trips.

• When Columbus was 25, the ship he was working on was attacked and destroyed. Columbus held on to an oar to keep himself afloat and swam six miles to Portugal.

• Columbus studied, sailed, and learned to read and write.

• In 1484, Columbus became commander of a ship.

Riddles:

Which bus crossed the ocean? (Columbus)

How do we know that Christopher Columbus was thrifty? (He traveled 30,000 miles on a galleon.)

Voyage Across the Ocean Sea

Book-Making Project

Materials _____

- ship pattern on page 97
- map on page 98
- writing paper
- 12" x18" (30.5 x 45.5 cm) blue construction paper
- 3" x 5" (7.5 x 13 cm) strip of blue paper
- scissors, glue
- stapler

1 Cut 5" (13 cm) off the end of the construction paper. Cut a wave pattern on one side of that piece. Cut writing paper that same size and shape.

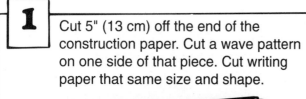

2 Reproduce the ship patterns. Color and cut out the patterns.

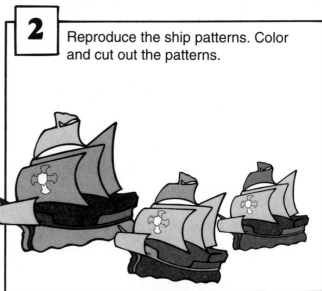

3 Staple student story and blue cover sheet to larger blue paper. Glue the strip of blue construction paper over the staples. Glue the three ships to the background sheet.

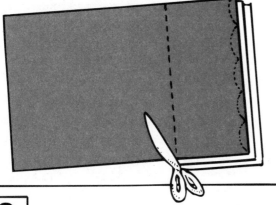

Glue the map to the back of the book. Draw lines to show Columbus' voyage(s).

Writing Suggestions _____

Describe Columbus' voyage from the point of view of one of his sailors.

- How would you feel sailing without knowing for sure where you were?

- What sights would you see?

- What sounds would you hear?

Support your writing with facts about the real voyage.

97

How to Make Books with Children EMC 578

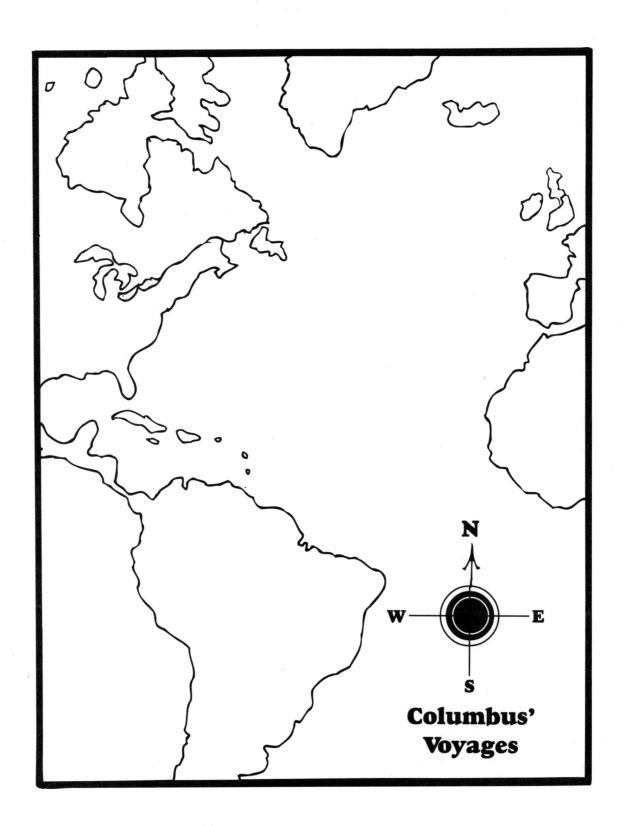

Columbus' Voyages

United Nations Day

October 24

Background

United Nations Day was first observed in 1947 on the second anniversary of the acceptance of the United Nations Charter. Today over 155 nations work together in the UN to preserve peace and benefit humankind. United Nations Day is celebrated in almost every country in the world. The purpose of the observance is to inform people of the UN's goals and achievements.

Books to Read

A Children's Chorus Introduction by Audrey Hepburn; E. P. Dutton, 1989.

Ruby Mae Has Something to Say by David Small; Crown Publishers, 1992.

The Story of the United Nations by R. Conrad Stein; Children's Press, 1986.

The United Nations by Adam Woog; Lucent Books, 1994.

United Nations by Carol Greene; Children's Press, 1983.

United Nations from A to Z by Nancy Winslow Parker; Dodd, Mead & Company, 1985.

Facts

- Before World War II ended, people all over the world believed that there should be an international peacekeeping organization that could prevent future wars. In October 1943, the foreign ministers of Great Britain, the Soviet Union, and the United States met in Moscow to discuss this goal. In the next year other nations joined the deliberations, and on October 24, 1945, the United Nations was born.

- More than 155 nations now send representatives to the U.N.'s headquarters in New York City.

The United Nations

An Individual Student Book

Materials

- U.N. Seal on page 101
- writing form on page 102
- 12" x 18" construction paper
- scissors and glue
- crayons or felt pens
- stapler

1 Fold the ends of the construction paper into the center.

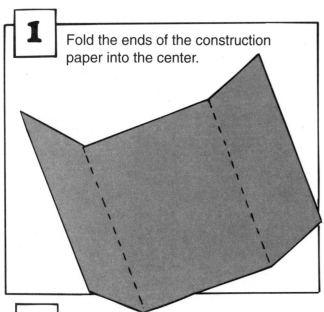

2 Cut the seal down the center and glue to the front flaps.

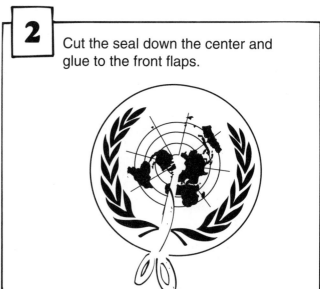

3 Staple student's essays inside the center section.

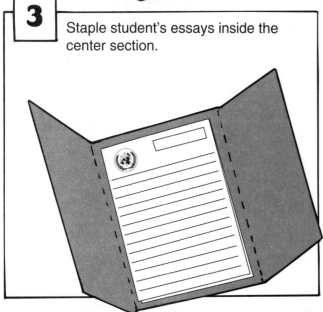

Writing Suggestions

The United Nations has many agencies that serve the world. Find out about these agencies.

Write an essay titled: Service to the World—The United Nations

 How to Make Books with Children EMC 578

How to Make Books with Children EMC 578

by:

_____

_____

_____

_____

_____

_____

_____

_____

_____

_____

_____

_____

_____

_____

_____

How to Make Books with Children EMC 578

Halloween

October 31

Background

Halloween is the eve of All Saints' Day, a feast celebrated by Roman Catholics. Long ago Halloween was called All-Hallows' Eve. It was a night when people believed that evil spirits roamed the earth. To protect themselves from harm, they kept huge bonfires going. They armed themselves with pitchforks and wore frightening clothes to ward off evil spirits.

Today, in many countries, Halloween is a children's holiday. Boys and girls of all ages wear weird masks and scary costumes and go from house to house shouting "Trick or Treat."

Books to Read

The Best Halloween of All by Susan Wojciechowski; Crown Publishers, 1992.

The Biggest Pumpkin Ever by Steven Kroll; Scholastic, 1984.

Boo! It's Halloween by Wendy Watson; Clarion Books, 1992.

The Great Pumpkin Switch by Megan McDonald; Orchard Books, 1992.

Halloween Party by Linda Shute; Lothrop, Lee & Shepard, 1994.

It's Pumpkin Time by Zoe Hall; Blue Sky Press, 1994.

Picnic at Mudsock Meadow by Patricia Polacco; Putnam, 1992.

Today Is Halloween by P. K. Hallinan; Forest House Publishing, 1992.

Facts

- In Ireland, pumpkins were hollowed out and used to light Halloween gatherings. The term jack-o-lantern is from an Irish legend about a man named Jack who was rejected by heaven because he was a miser and by hell because he had played jokes on the devil and so eternally traveled earth lighting his way with a lantern.

- Originally, people in England and Ireland carved beets, potatoes, and turnips as well as pumpkins.

- Scotch and Irish girls *wet the sark sleeve* on Halloween. Girls washed fine pieces of linen and hung them before the fire at eleven. At twelve, the images of their future husbands were supposed to appear on the cloths.

- In Wales, children go from house to house asking for apples, pears, plums, and cherries. In France children beg for flowers.

Growing Pumpkins

An Individual Student Book

Materials _____

- 4 copies of the pop-up pattern on page 106
- picture cards on page 105
- scissors, glue
- felt pens or crayons
- 9" x 12" (23 x 30.5 cm) colored construction paper for the cover

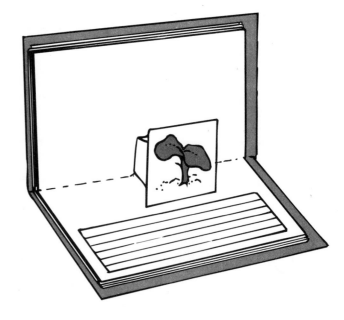

1 Cut and fold the pop-up pattern for each of the four pieces.

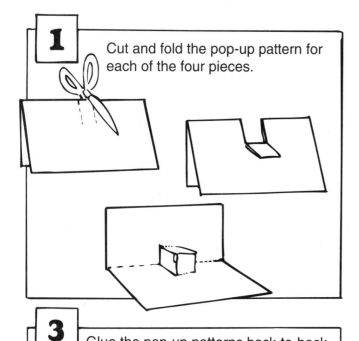

2 Color, cut, and glue one of the picture cards on each tab. Describe each step in the writing area.

3 Glue the pop-up patterns back-to-back. (See pop-up binding page 3) Glue these pages into the folded construction paper cover.

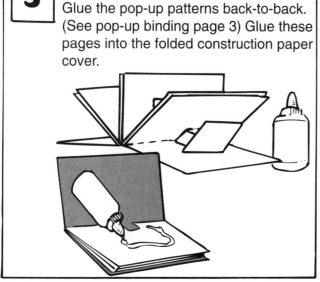

Writing Suggestions _____

Tell how a pumpkin grows. Be sure to put the steps in the correct order.

How to Make Books with Children EMC 578

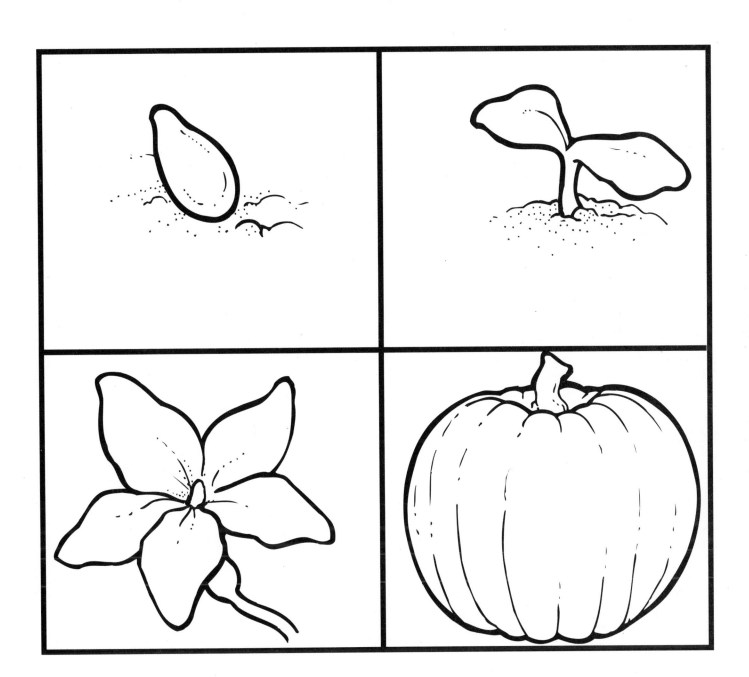

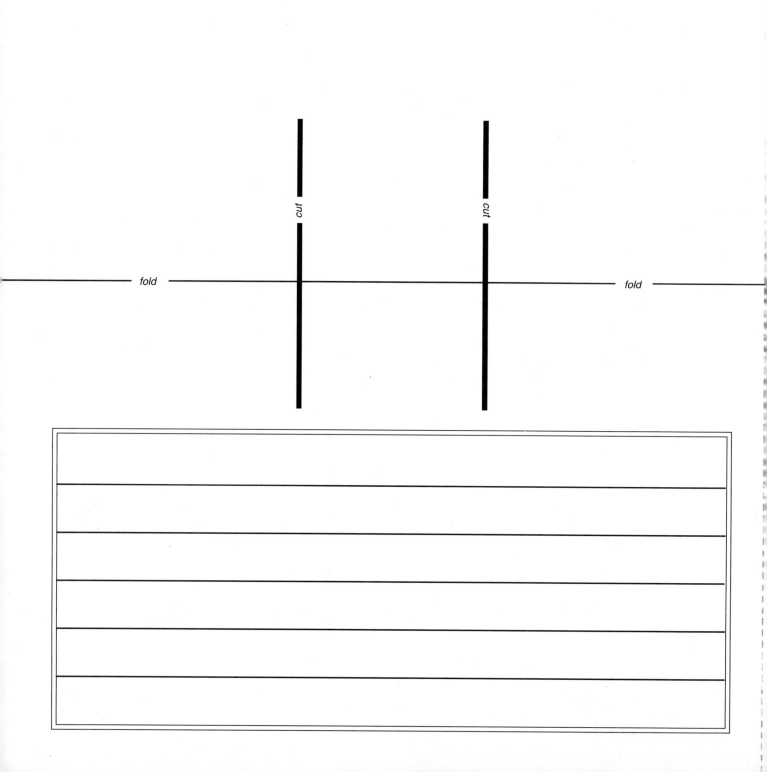

Night Flyers

Book-Making Project

Materials

- bat pattern on page 108
- 9" x 12" (23 x 30.5 cm) black construction paper
- 12" x 12" (30.5 x 30.5 cm) blue construction paper
- writing paper
- small gold star stickers
- paper scraps
- scissors, glue
- stapler

1 Cut out and color the bat. Cut writing paper to match the shape of the bat pattern.

2 Staple the bat cover to each finished story. Glue the last sheet of writing paper to the blue paper. Add gold stars to the sky.

3 Add a cover and staple all stories together. Fold and glue a strip of paper over the staples. Cut and glue a moon from white paper.

Add a title.

Writing Suggestions

- Learn about the nocturnal habits of bats.
- Write about one evening with a bat.

How to Make Books with Children EMC 578

Who's Inside?
A Class Book

Materials

- pattern on page 110
- 4" x 9" (10 x 23 cm) writing paper
- 12" x 15" (30.5 x 38 cm) light blue construction paper
- scissors, glue
- felt pens or crayons
- pencil
- hole punch and black yarn

1

Fold over 5" (13 cm) on the side of the blue paper. Glue the writing paper on the flap. Glue the top flap of the ghost to the paper.

2

Trace around the ghost with a pencil. Lift up the "ghost flap" and draw yourself under the sheet.

3

Bind all student stories together. Add a cover and punch two holes. Insert yarn. Add two jack-o-lanterns at the end of the yarn pieces.

who is inside?

Writing Suggestions

Who is inside the ghost costume?

1. Students draw themselves inside and then write a few clues.

2. Post the ghosts. Try to guess before lifting the flaps.

Put glue on back
of folded section

fold

How to Make Books with Children EMC 578

Thanksgiving

The fourth Thursday in November

Background

Thanksgiving is a day to give thanks for the harvest and for other blessings of the past year. Thanksgiving was first observed by the Pilgrims in 1621 in celebration of their first harvest. Governor Bradford of Plymouth Colony ordered the day for feasting and thanks. It was proclaimed a national holiday by President Washington in 1789.

Books to Read

It's Thanksgiving by Jack Prelutsky; Scholastic, 1982.

Oh, What a Thanksgiving by Steven Kroll; Scholastic, 1988.

Over the River and Through the Woods by Lydia Maria Child; Scholastic, 1974.

Thanksgiving Treat by Catherine Stock; Bradbury Press, 1990.

Three Young Pilgrims by Cheryl Harness; Aladdin Paperbacks, 1992.

A Turkey for Thanksgiving by Eve Bunting; Clarion Books, 1991.

'Twas the Night Before Thanksgiving by David Pilkey; Orchard Books, 1990.

Facts

• The first Thanksgiving feast lasted for three days.

• Eighteen Pilgrim women crossed the Atlantic on the Mayflower. They had no voice or vote in what happened.

• Two babies were born enroute.

• After one winter in America there were only six women alive.

• Thirty children were part of the original Pilgrim Party.

• The Pilgrims' houses were built of sawed pine boards.

• The first building built by the Pilgrims was a storehouse that became a hospital.

The Gift of Corn

An Individual Student Book

Materials _____

- 3 or 4 corn writing forms on page 113
- 4 1/2" x 8 1/2" (11.5 X 21.5 cm) yellow construction paper
- 4 1/2" x 8 1/2" (11.5 X 21.5 cm) green construction paper
- hole punch
- crayons or felt pens
- scissors, glue
- paper fastener

1 Cut 2 yellow construction paper cover pieces to match the shape of the writing form. Add details with felt pen.

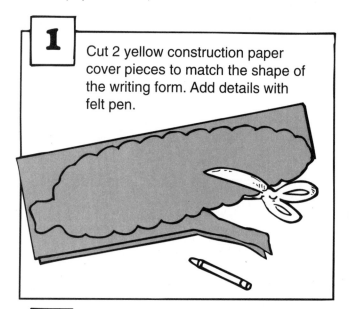

2 Cut green construction paper for the leaves. Put all the layers together, punch a hole, and fasten with a paper fastener.

3 Write the title of the story on the yellow construction paper cover.

Writing Suggestions _____

Corn is an important crop in the United States today.

Write about:
1. How corn grows.
2. How we use corn.
3. Why corn was so important to the Pilgrims.

How to Make Books with Children EMC 578

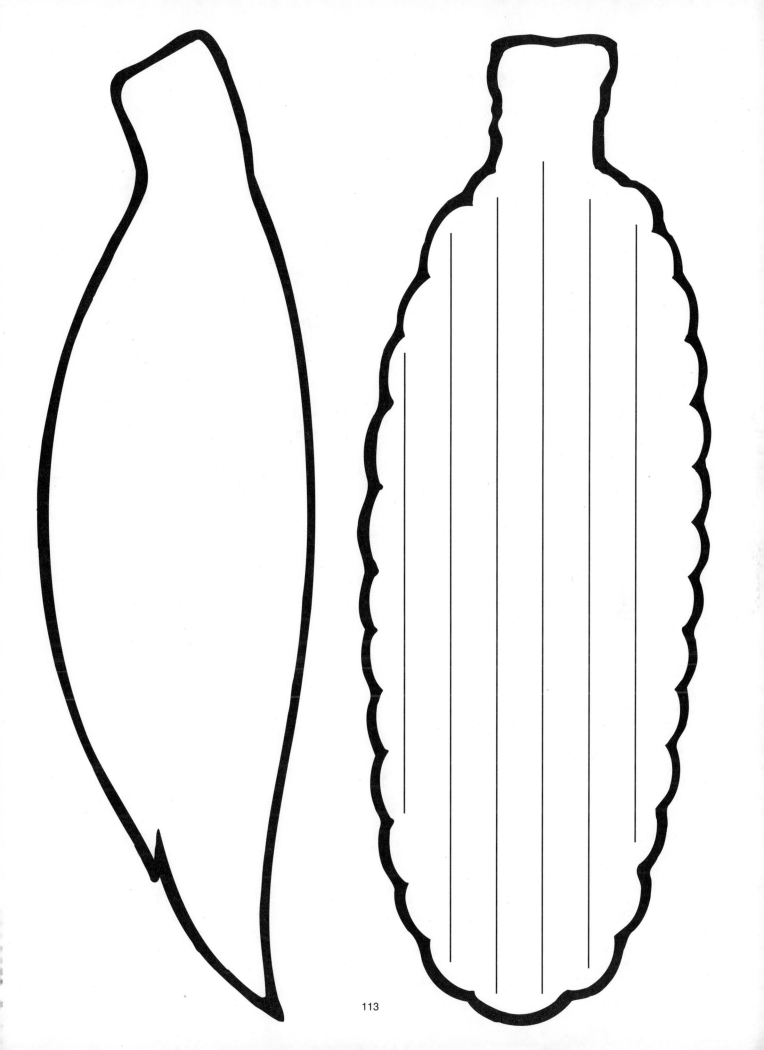

Thanksgiving Turkey
A Class Book

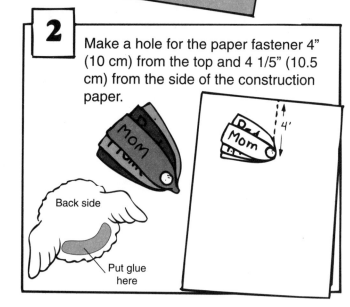

Materials _____

- patterns on pages 115-116
- 9" x 12" (23 x 30.5 cm) construction paper
- paper fastener
- scissors, glue
- crayons or felt pens
- hole punch
- twine

1

Cut out and color all pattern pieces. Write something to be thankful for on each feather. Attach the feathers together with the paper fastener.

2

Make a hole for the paper fastener 4" (10 cm) from the top and 4 1/5" (10.5 cm) from the side of the construction paper.

Back side

Put glue here

3

Place the turkey body over the paper fastener. Fold back the flap of the turkey head and glue that to the body. Glue the title box below.

Bind all pages together by punching holes and tying with twine.

Writing Suggestions _____

Thanksgiving is a time to be thankful.

- List all the things that you are thankful for.

- Copy the most important things on the feathers of the turkey.

- Then write a note that tells why you feel the way you do.

fold

paste

How to Make Books with Children EMC 578

I am so thankful

_____

_____

_____

_____

_____

116 How to Make Books with Children EMC 578

Look Who Came to Dinner

A Class Book

Materials

- pattern on page 118
- scissors
- crayons or felt pens
- 2 sheets of 9" x 12" (23 x 30.5 cm) construction paper for cover
- 4" x 12" (10 x 30.5 cm) construction paper strip
- stapler

1

Draw someone who came to the original Thanksgiving. The head must be in the top section, the torso in the mid-section and the legs in the bottom section.

2

Staple all student papers to the construction paper. Cut along the gray lines. Turn different sections and create funny combinations.

3

Staple a front cover to the book. Cover the staples with a folded strip of construction paper. Add the title.

Writing Suggestions

- Give your Thanksgiving characters names.

- Tell what they brought to the first Thanksgiving Dinner.

- Write about what they were thankful for.

117   How to Make Books with Children EMC 578

Look who came to dinner!

_____

name of guest

by _____

neck

What did they bring:

What were they thankful for?

St. Nicholas Day

December 5 or 6

Background

St. Nicholas, a bishop in Asia Minor in the fourth century, is the patron saint of children and sailors. In many European countries, St. Nicholas is remembered on December 6. Children leave their shoes out in hopes of receiving treats. St. Nicholas, dressed differently in different countries, travels through towns and villages with his servant and his little donkey, filling the shoes with small gifts. Traditionally in the Netherlands, children left their wooden shoes out to be filled.

Books to Read

The Legend of St. Nicholas by Verena Morgenthaler; H. Z. Walck, 1970.

A Gift from St. Nicholas adapted by Carole Kismaric; Holiday House, 1988.

Christmas in Today's Germany by World Book, Inc., 1996.

Merry Christmas—Children at Christmastime Around the World by Robina Beckles Willson; Plihomel Books, 1983.

Facts

• St. Nicholas is said to have brought three murdered schoolboys back to life with love and prayers.

• The Bishop Nicholas gave a nobleman dowries for his three daughters. He tossed the bags of gold into the house. The third bag of gold fell into a stocking hung by the chimney to dry.

• St. Nicholas travels with his helper, Black Peter. Black Peter puts coal in shoes of those who have been bad.

• Children leave carrots and hay in their shoes for St. Nicholas' horse. The next morning the shoes will hold candies and presents if the children have been good.

 How to Make Books with Children EMC 578

Wooden Shoe

A Class Book

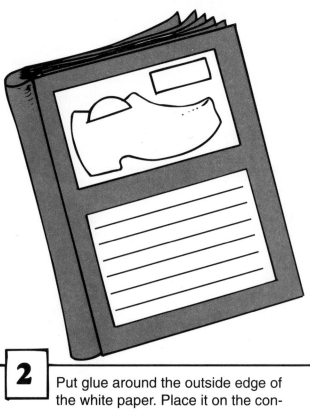

Materials _____

- shoe pattern on page 121
- pull tab pattern on page 122
- 12" x 18" (30.5 x 45.5 cm) construction paper
- 8 1/2" x 7" (21.5 x 18 cm) writing paper
- scissors and glue
- crayons or felt tip pens
- hole punch
- shoelace

1 Cut out the pull tab pattern. Draw St. Nicholas' surprise in the box. Cut the slit in the shoe. Slip the pull-tab through the slit.

2 Put glue around the outside edge of the white paper. Place it on the construction paper.

3 Put all student papers together. Punch two holes and bind the stories together with a shoelace.

Glue a copy of the small wooden shoe pattern on the cover for each student who contributes a story.

Writing Suggestions _____

What did St. Nicholas leave in the shoe? Why did he leave what he did? Write a story to explain.

How to Make Books with Children EMC 578

Happy St. Nicholas Day

by: _____

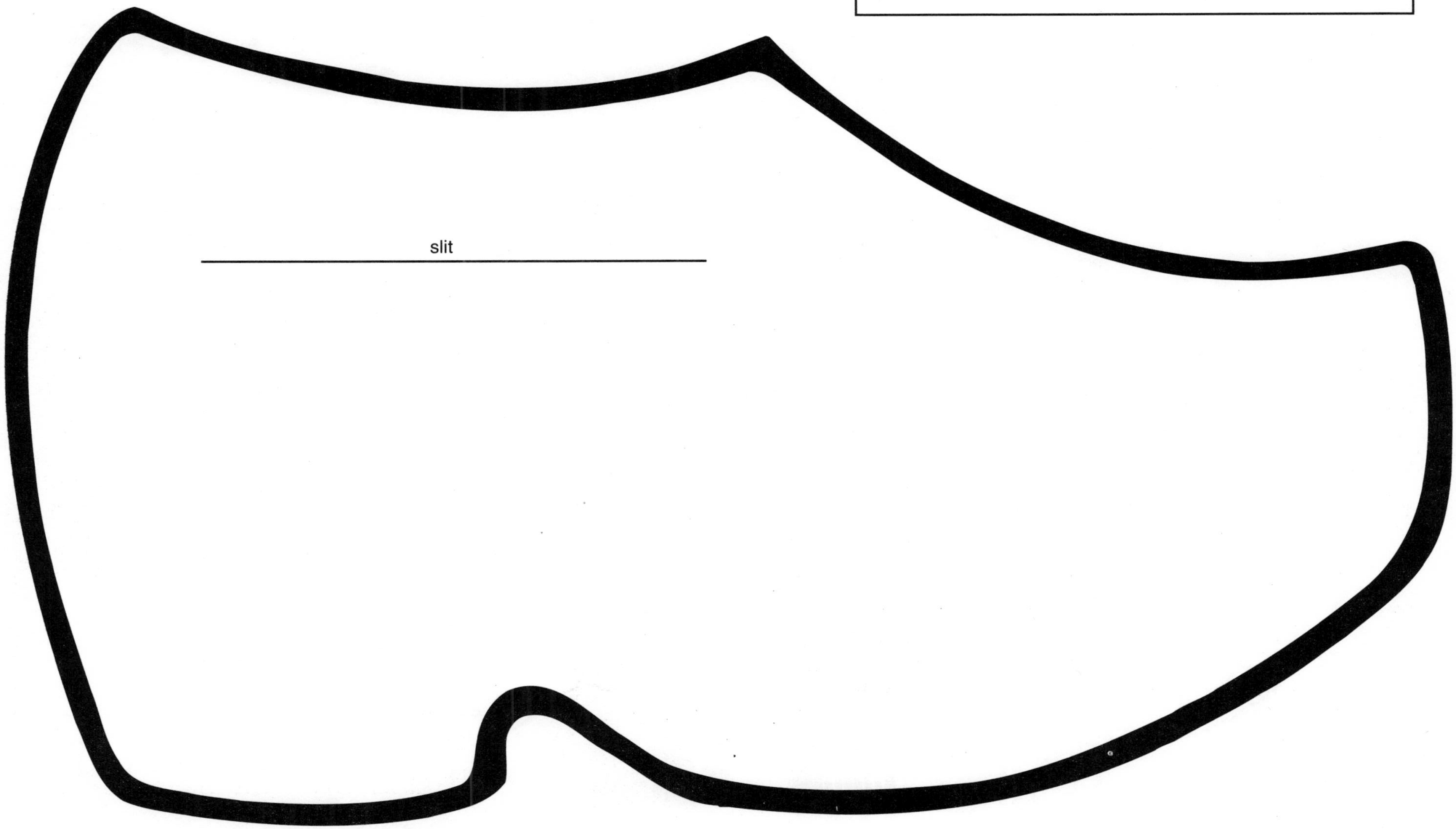

slit

How to Make Books with Children EMC 578

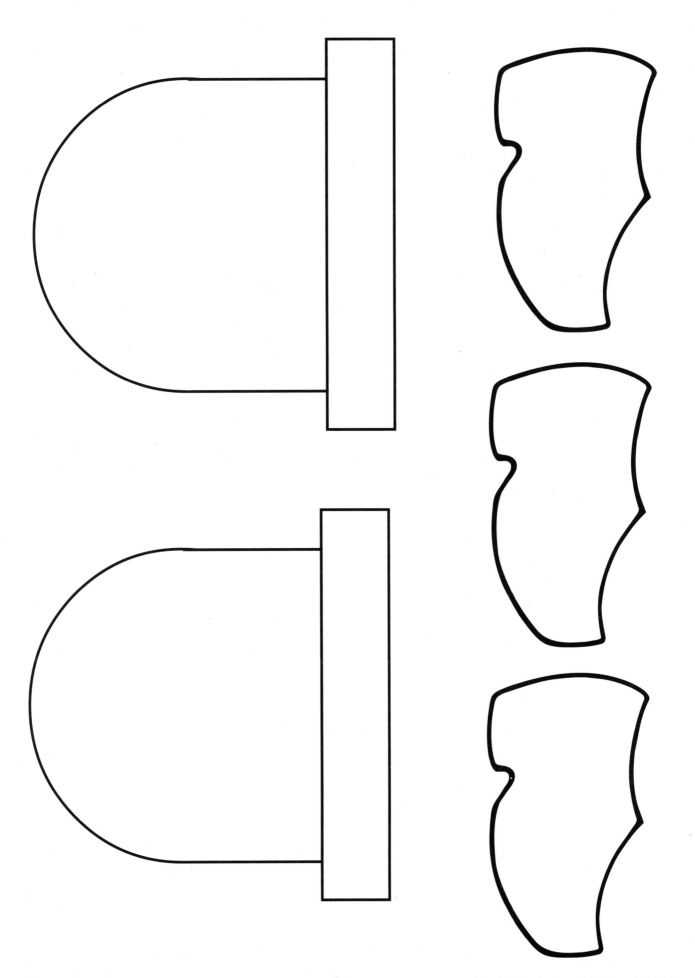

How to Make Books with Children EMC 578

La Posada

December 16-24

Background

In Mexico, beginning on December 16 and for the next nine days, through December 24, Posadas processions reenact Mary and Joseph's search for lodging in Bethlehem. A parade of children, carrying lanterns and platforms with figures of Mary and Joseph, stops at homes of neighbors and begs to be taken in. When they reach a prearranged house, the manger is carried in, prayers said, and refreshments served. A piñata is often the highlight of the social part of the celebration.

Books to Read

Nine Days to Christmas by Marie Hall Ets and Aurora Labastida; Viking Press, 1959.

Pancho's Piñata by Stefan Czernecki and Timothy Rhodes; Hyperion Books for Children, 1992.

Facts

Posada means an inn or place of lodging.

La Posada

An Individual Student Book

Materials _____

- donkey pattern on page 125
- writing form and lantern on page 126
- 9" x 12" (23 x 30.5 cm) dark blue construction paper
- 4" x 12" (10 x 30.5 cm) brown construction paper
- 4" x 12" (10 x 30.5 cm) writing paper
- 3" x 4" (7.5 x 10 cm) brown construction paper strip
- gold star stickers
- 3" (7.5 cm) piece of string
- scissors, glue, stapler, tape

Writing Suggestions _____

Write a question and answer book.

Is there room for us here?
Sorry, we have no room.

Is there room for us here?
We have no room.

Is there room for us here?
We welcome you!

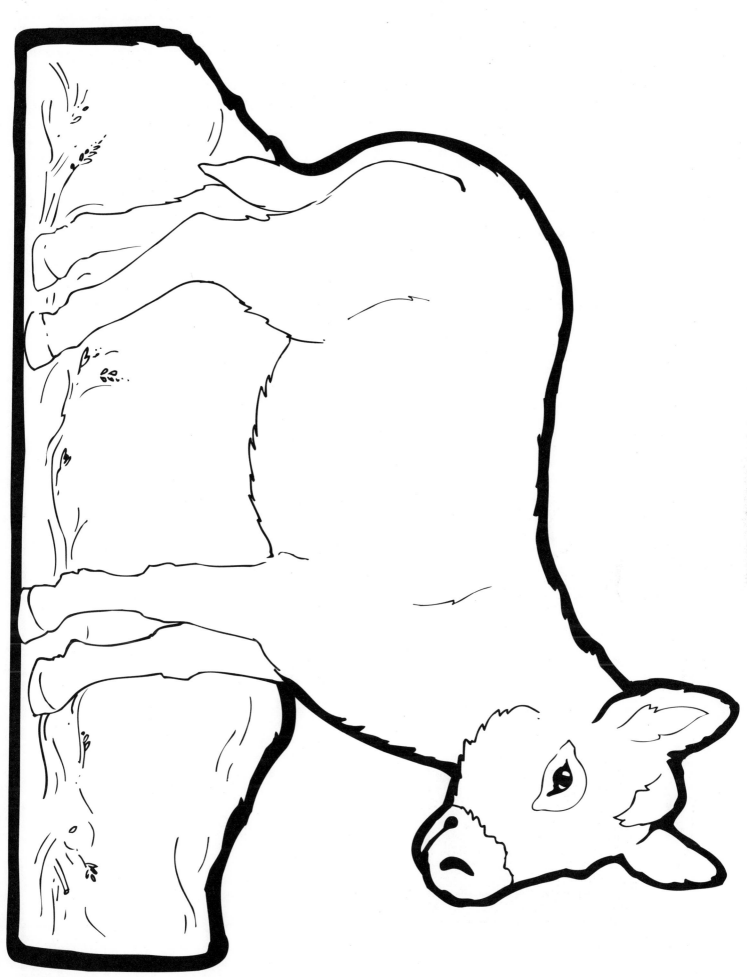

How to Make Books with Children EMC 578

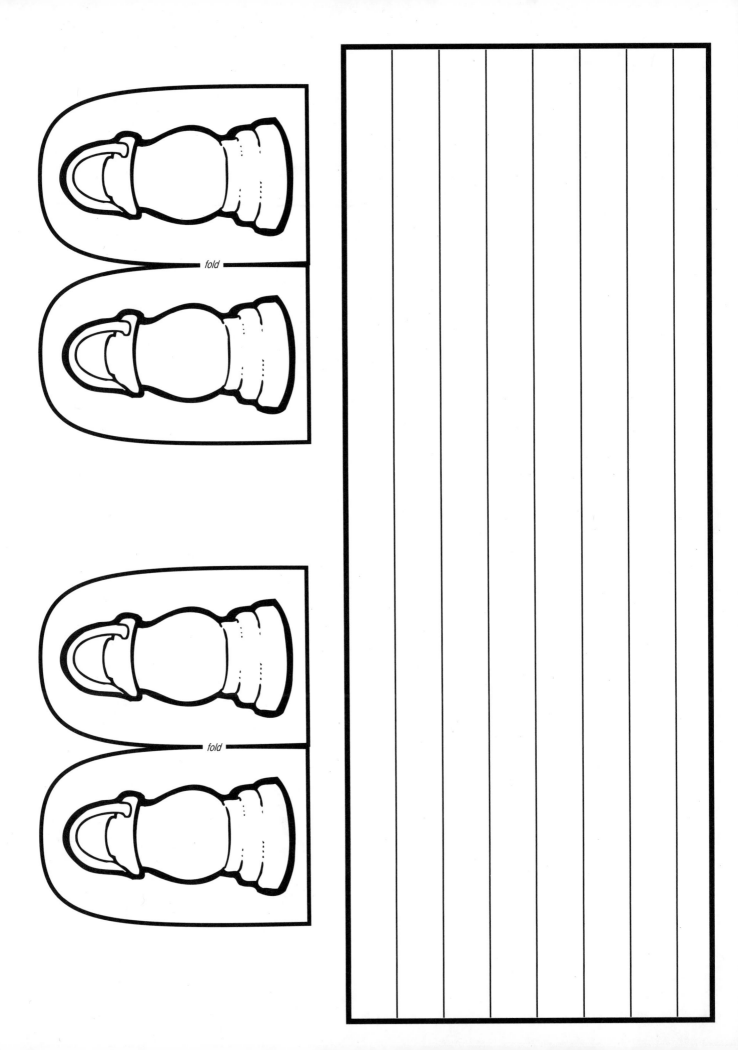

fold

fold

St. Lucia Day

December 13

Background

On the shortest, darkest day of winter all Sweden rejoices in a festival of light called St. Lucia Day. At daybreak, in every home, a girl dressed in sparkling white pretends to be Lucia, Queen of Lights. She reminds everyone that soon in this northern country the days will be longer. Traditionally "Lucia" is the oldest daughter in the house and wears a long white robe with a bright red sash. On her head she wears a beautiful crown of evergreens decked with candles. Aglow with lights, she serves coffee and special holiday buns.

Books to Read

A Calf for Christmas by Astrid Lindgren; R & S Books, 1991.

Lucia, Child of Light by Florence Ekstrand; Welcome Press, 1989.

Sweden by Delice Gan Cheng Fun; Marshall Cavendish Corp., 1992.

Facts

- Lucia was a young girl who lived in Sicily around 300 A.D. She was blinded and executed by the Romans because she would not give up her belief in the Christian religion.

- *Lucia* means light.

- Young boys wear white cone-shaped caps decorated with stars and follow Lucia in the procession.

- The Lucia processions thank the Queen of Light for bringing hope at the darkest time of the year.

St. Lucia

An Individual Student Book

Materials _____

- pop-up pattern on page 129
- Lucia pattern on page 130
- 9" x 12" (23 x 30.5 cm) construction paper
- scissors, glue
- crayons or felt pens

---

1 Fold and cut the pop-up pattern.

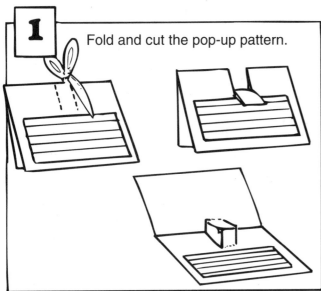

2 Color and cut out St. Lucia. Glue her to the pop-up tab.

3 Fold the construction paper in half. Lay the pop-up in the folder. Put glue around the edge of the paper. Close the folder and press. Glue the other side too. (See pop-up hints, page 3).

Writing Suggestions _____

Think about a day with no sunlight. Write about how it would make you feel.

Sit in the sun and then describe the way the warm rays change your feelings.

Then write a summary of the "Festival of Light." Use your observations about how light and dark make you feel to help explain why the holiday is celebrated.

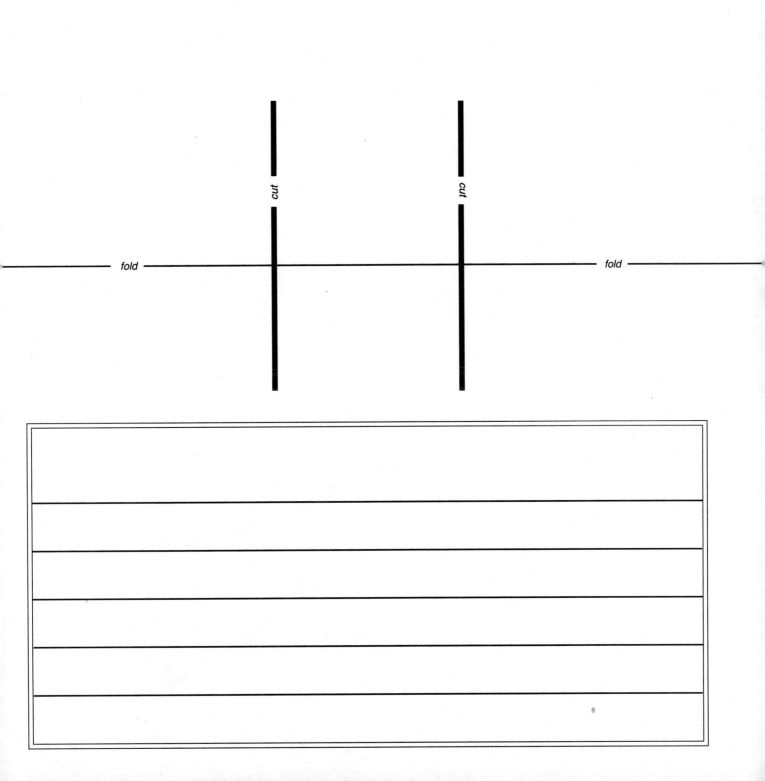

cut

cut

fold

fold

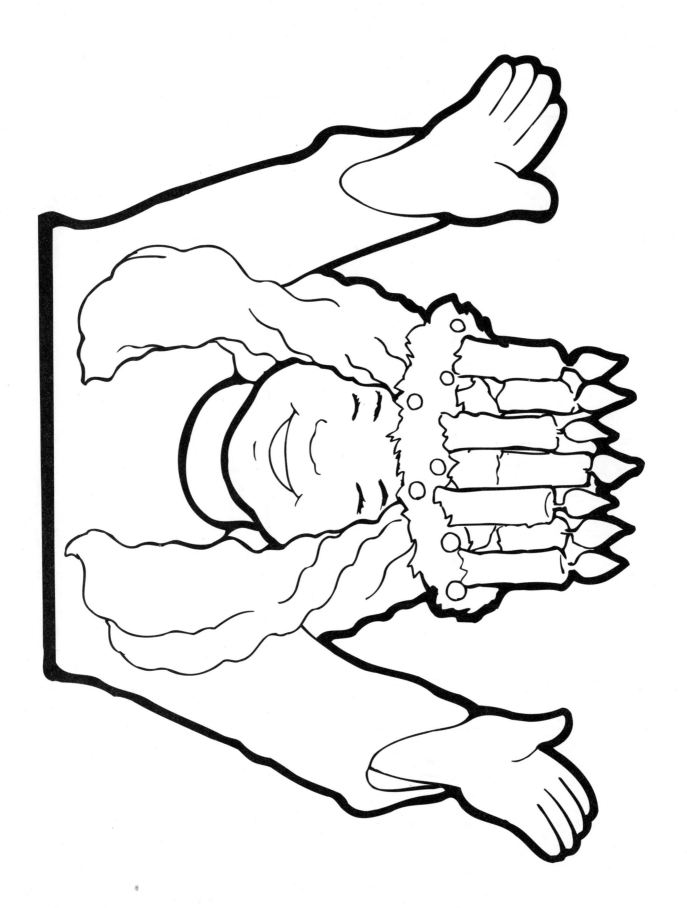

Bill of Rights Day

December 15

Background

The Bill of Rights—the first ten amendments to the Constitution — was ratified on December 15, 1791. It describes fundamental rights guaranteed to every American. President Franklin D. Roosevelt proclaimed the celebration of Bill of Right's Day in 1941 just eight days after the Japanese attack on Pearl Harbor. The celebration is meant to reaffirm every American's basic rights.

Books to Read

The Bill of Rights by Warren Colman; Children's Press, 1987.

The Bill of Rights: How We Got It and What It Means by Milton Meltzer; Thomas Crowell, 1990.

Shh! We're Writing the Constitution by Jean Fritz; Putnam, 1987.

Facts

Bill of Rights

(Constitutional Amendments 1-10)

1. Freedom of religion, speech, press; right to assemble and petition

2. The right to bear arms

3. Soldiers cannot be housed in private homes without consent

4. Citizens and their belongings cannot be seized and searched without proper cause

5. Laws concerning prosecution, such as not being tried twice for the same crime

6. The right to a speedy public trial

7. The right to a trial by jury

8. Prohibits "cruel and unusual" punishment

9. People are granted rights not listed in Constitution as long as they are not denied by law.

10. Powers not specifically given to the federal government belong to the states

The Bill of Rights Scroll

A Class Book

Materials

- scroll writing form on page 133
- shelf paper
- ribbon
- glue

1 Cut out the scroll pattern. Cut the shelf paper long enough to hold the writing form.

2 Glue the Bill of Rights scroll pattern to the shelf paper.

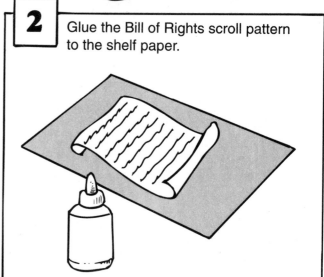

3 Roll up the shelf paper and tie with the ribbon.

Writing Suggestions

The men who wrote the Bill of Rights recognized the need to guarantee certain privileges to every citizen. Write a Bill of Rights for your classroom. Make sure that every student agrees with what is written. Have the document signed by all its authors.

How to Make Books with Children EMC 578

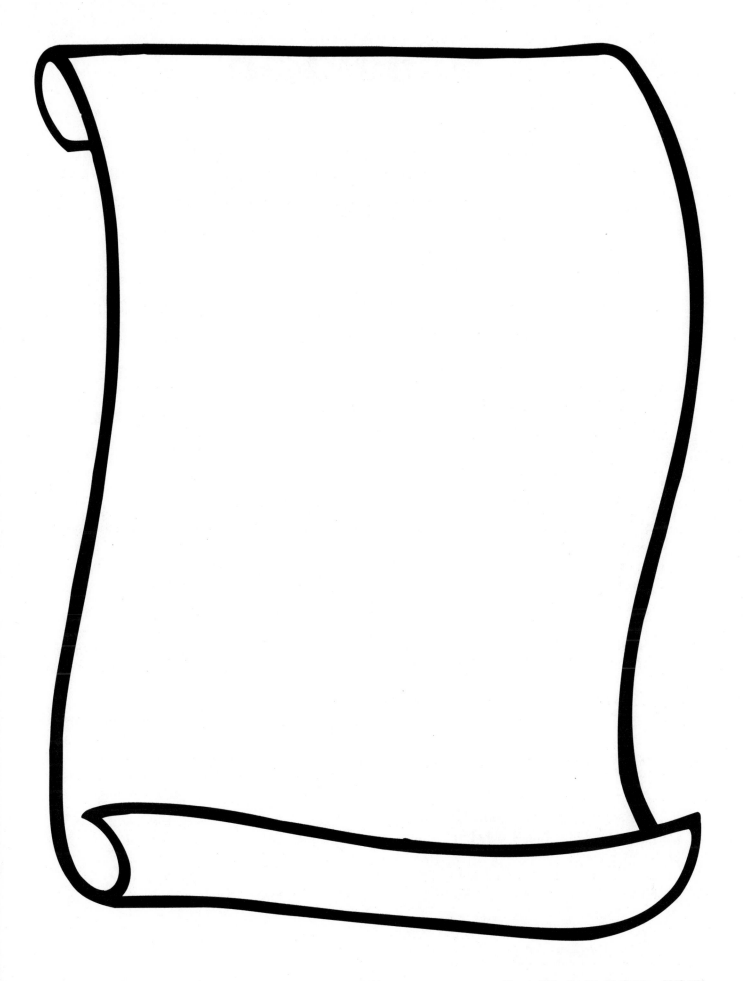

133

Hanukkah

Background

Hanukkah may have been celebrated as early as 165BC. It begins on the twenty fifth day of the Jewish month of Kislev. It lasts for eight days in celebration of the miracle that occurred when the Eternal Light in the temple stayed lit for eight days with only one day's supply of oil.

Each night families get together to light the Hanukkah Menorah, an eight-branched candelabrum. The first night only one candle is lit. Each night one more candle is added. The last night all eight Hanukkah candles burn in windows all over the country.

Everyone loves the potato pancakes (latkes), games, and singing that are a part of the holiday. Children receive gifts of money and play with a square-sided top called a *dreidel.*

Books to Read

All the Lights in the Night by Arthur Levine; Tambourine Books, 1991.

Elijah's Angel by Michael J. Rosen; Harcourt Brace Jovanovich, 1992.

Hershel and the Hanukkah Goblins by Eric Kimmel; Holiday House, 1985.

In the Month of Kislev by Nina Jaffe; Viking Press, 1992.

Latkes and Applesauce by Frank Manushkin; Scholastic, 1989.

The Miracle of the Potato Latkes by Malka Penn; Holiday House, 1994.

One Yellow Daffodil by David A. Adler; Gulliver Books, 1995.

The Spotted Pony retold by Eric Kimmel; Holiday House, 1992.

Facts

- Judah the Maccabee fought the Syrians for three years. When he and his men finally defeated the Syrians, they reclaimed their temple.

- The temple was cleaned and Jewish soldiers relit the menorah. They had only enough oil for one day and knew that it would take eight days to get more oil.

- Incredibly, that oil lasted for the eight days. Hanukkah celebrates this miracle and the rededication of the temple.

The Dreidel

A Three-fold Book-Making Project

Materials

- dreidel patterns on pages 136 and 137
- 12" x 18" (30.5 x 45.5 cm) construction paper
- glue and scissors
- crayons or felt pens

1 Fold the construction paper into thirds.

2 Cut out the dreidel writing pattern. Glue it to the paper. Cut around the top and bottom edge. Do not cut the sides.

3 Open the first flap of the book. Glue the first two boxes that tell about 2 sides of the dreidel. Open the other flap and glue the last two boxes.

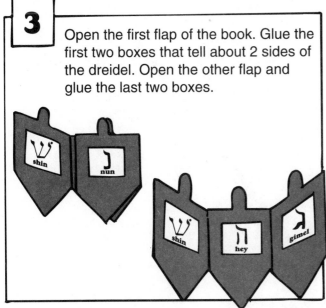

Writing Suggestions

Review the rules of the Dreidel game. Then write directions for playing the game.

To play you will need: 1 dreidel
1 cup
peanuts or raisins

Every player has a handful of peanuts or raisins. Each player puts one raisin or peanut in the cup. The first player spins the dreidel. Whichever symbol lands face up indicates whether the player takes everything, takes half, or takes nothing from the cup. If shin (give) lands up, everyone puts in another nut or raisin. Each player takes a turn following the rules.

135

How to Make Books with Children EMC 578

The Dreidel

How to play

_____

_____

_____

_____

_____

_____

by: _____

_____

gimel
everything

shin
give

hey
half

nun
nothing

How to Make Books with Children EMC 578

Christmas

December 25

Background

Christmas is one of the world's most loved holidays: a day to sing carols, exchange presents, and celebrate with family. For Christians, Christmas honors the birth of Christ nearly 2,000 years ago.

For centuries, people have celebrated Christmas with the giving of gifts. In Spain, children believe that three wise men bring them gifts. In Russia, a good witch named Babouska sneaks into houses to slip gifts under children's pillows. Swedish children wait for Jultomten, a present-giving elf, while German children place baskets by their front doors so the Christkindl will fill them with cookies and candy. In England, Santa Claus is called Father Christmas. Polish children wait for the Star Man, and in France Pere Noel brings presents to children on Christmas Day.

Books to Read

The Christmas Ark by Robert D. San Souci; Doubleday, 1991.

The Christmas Day Kitten by James Herriot; St. Martin's Press, 1986.

The Christmas Miracle of Johnathan Toomey by Susan Wojciechowski; Candlewick Press, 1995.

The Grinch Who Stole Christmas by Dr. Seuss; Random House, 1957.

Santa's Book of Names by David McPhail; Little, Brown, 1993.

Thank You, Santa by Margaret Wild; Scholastic, 1991.

The Wild Christmas Reindeer by Jan Brett; Putnam, 1990.

Facts

- The people of Germany and Scandinavia were the first to bring Christmas trees into their homes.

- In Sweden many children make straw billy goats to guard their trees against evil spirits that might steal the decorations.

- Most trees in the U.S. are grown on Christmas Tree farms and shipped all over the country. It takes about eight years to grow an average-sized tree.

The Nine Reindeer

An Individual Student Book

Materials

- reindeer pattern on page 140
- 9 copies of writing form on page 141
- 3 sheets of brown 12" x 18" (30.5 x 45.5 cm) construction paper
- paper scraps
- scissors, glue
- tape

1

Fold each sheet of brown paper into thirds. Lay the reindeer pattern on the top and trace around it. Cut the top and bottom edge through all three layers. Do not cut the sides.

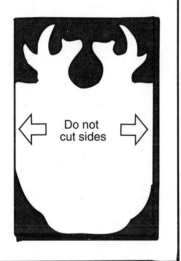

Do not cut sides

2

Tape the three brown paper sections together. Use felt pen or paper scraps to add eyes, ears, and noses to the nine reindeer.

3

Glue the story in correct order on the backs of the reindeer.

Writing Suggestions

Take a reindeer's point of view and describe the Christmas Eve journey.

- How does it feel to fly through the air pulling a sleigh?

- What is it like to deliver toys around the world?

- What problems did Santa and his team have to overcome?

140

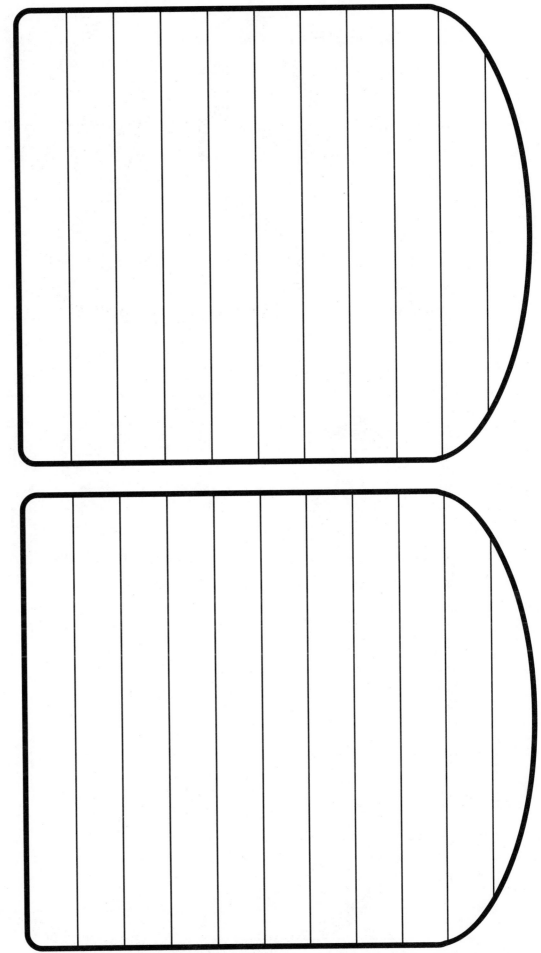

How to Make Books with Children EMC 578

A Christmas Tree

A Class Book

Materials

- tree pattern on page 143
- writing form on page 144
- scissors, glue
- crayons or felt pens
- 12" x 18" (39.5 x 45.5 cm) construction paper
- hole punch
- Christmas ribbon

1 Color, decorate, and cut out the tree.

2 Glue the tree and the writing form on the construction paper.

3 Bind student stories together. Punch holes in the left margin and secure the pages with pieces of brightly colored ribbon.

Writing Suggestions

Practice descriptive writing by describing your Christmas Tree and your favorite ornaments. Use words that help the readers to "see" what you are writing about.

How to Make Books with Children EMC 578

How to Make Books with Children EMC 578

Santa's Pack

A Class Book

Materials

- writing paper form on page 146
- 2 sheets of 9" x 12" (23 x 30.5 cm) brown construction paper
- scissors, glue
- crayons or felt pens
- ribbon
- hole punch and a pencil
- 2 paper fasteners

1

Cut out the writing form. Trace 1/4" (.6 cm) larger than the form on the brown paper. Place both brown sheets together and cut along the pencil line. If you wish, cut pieces of plain white paper in the shape of the pack for illustrations.

2

Place all student writing forms inside the cover. Punch two holes on the bottom edge and secure with paper fasteners.

3

Put a title on the cover. Tie a ribbon around the top of the book.

Writing Suggestions

Describe what is in Santa's pack.

Take Santa's point of view...
- Explain why you deliver gifts to so many children.

- Tell why you chose a certain gift for a specific child.

- Describe any problems you have with the elves and the reindeer and how you solved them.

         How to Make Books with Children EMC 578

Kwanzaa

December 26

Background

Kwanzaa is a Swahili word that means "first fruits." This holiday was started in 1966 to celebrate African-American heritage. Kwanzaa lasts for seven days.

During Kwanzaa, families light candles in a candle holder called a *kinara*. Each day of Kwanzaa has a special meaning or principle. At the end of the seven days, children receive African or handmade gifts. Families and friends enjoy a feast, sing songs, play music, and share stories of their family history.

Books to Read

Celebrating Kwanzaa by Diane Hoyt-Goldsmith; Holiday House, 1993.

It's Kwanzaa Time by Linda and Clay Goss; Putnam, 1995.

Kwanzaa Karamu by April A. Brady; Carolrhoda Books, 1995.

My First Kwanzaa Book by Deborah M. Newton Chocolate; Scholastic, 1992.

Seven Candles for Kwanzaa by Andrea Davis Pinkney; Dial Books for Young Readers, 1993.

Facts

The Seven Principles of Kwanzaa

1. *Umoja* (Oo-moe-jah) unity

2. *Kujich aguilia* (Koo-gee-cha-goo-tee-ah) self determination

3. *Ujima* (Oo-gee-mah) collective work and responsibility

4. *Ujamaa* (Oo-jah-mah) cooperative economics

5. *Nia* (Nee-ah) purpose

6. *Kuumba* (Koom-bah) creativity

7. *Imani* (Ee-mahn-e) faith

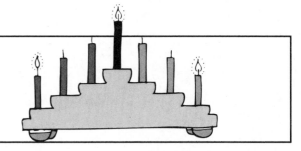

There are three red candles on the left, one black candle in the center, and three green ones on the right. Usually the black candle is lit on the first night. Then red and green are alternated.

The Kinara

An Individual Student Book

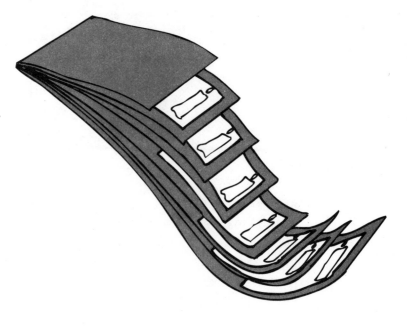

Materials

- writing forms on page 149. Each student will need 7 forms
- 4 strips of 3" x 18" (15 x 45.5 cm) black construction paper
- scissors, glue
- ruler
- crayons or felt pens
- stapler

1 Lay the black strips of paper down in a graduated sequence leaving 1 1/2" (3.5 cm) at the right side of each strip. Make a pencil mark at the last strip.

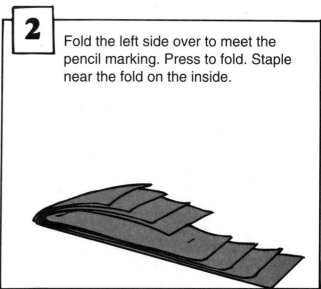

2 Fold the left side over to meet the pencil marking. Press to fold. Staple near the fold on the inside.

3 Glue a candle pattern on each segment. Save the top layer as the title flap. Color (light) a new candle each day, and write about the principle it represents. *(Use the Kwanzaa Kinara diagram on page 147 to see the color of the candles and the order in which they are lit.)*

Writing Suggestions

Write about each of the principles of Kwanzaa. Tell what they mean in your daily life.

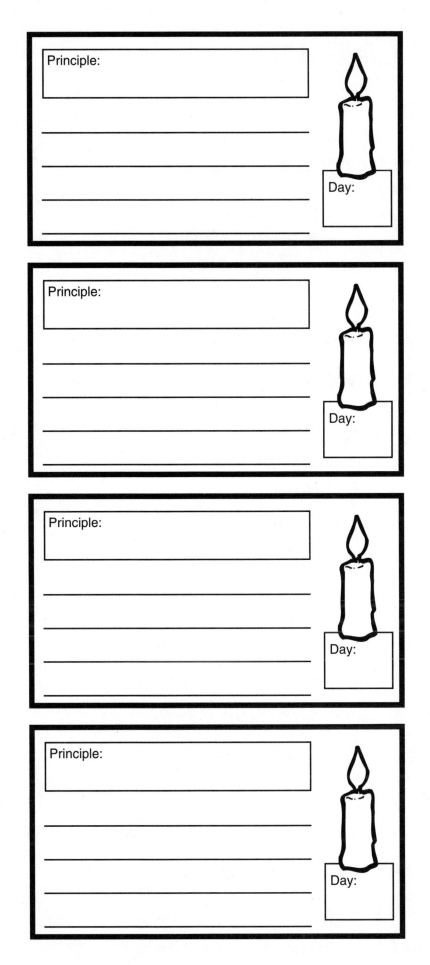

Principle:

_____

_____

_____

_____

Day:

Principle:

_____

_____

_____

Day:

Principle:

_____

_____

_____

Day:

Principle:

_____

_____

_____

Day:

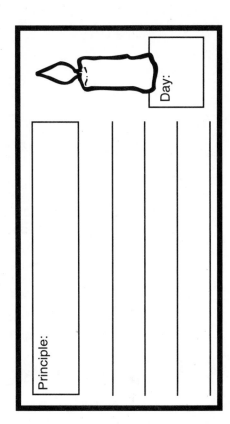

Day:

Principle:

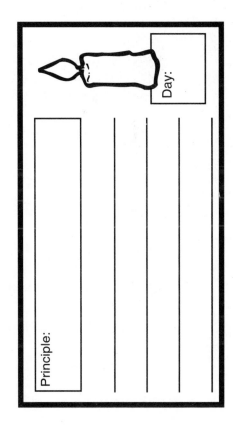

Day:

Principle:

Birthdays

Every day of the year

Background

Long ago at a child's birth, a baby was surrounded by friends and good wishes to scare away evil spirits. Birthday parties probably were first given in Germany where kinderfestes (children's celebrations) were held on the anniversary of a child's birth. Birthday cakes with candles were also a German tradition. The candles were thought to have magic qualities.

The traditional *Happy Birthday* song was written around 1900 by two Americans, Mildred J. and Patty S. Hill. The song is an American tradition that has spread around the world.

Books to Read

Angelina's Birthday Surprise by Katharine Holabird; Clarkson N. Potter, 1989.

A Birthday Basket for Tia by Pat Mora; Macmillan, 1992.

The Birthday Moon by Lois Duncan; Viking Kestel, 1989.

The Birthday Thing by SuAnn Kiser; Greenwillow Books, 1989.

A Flower Garden by Eve Bunting; Harcourt Brace, 1994.

Happy Birthday to You by Dr. Seuss; Random House, 1959.

Henry and Mudge and the Best Day of All by Cynthia Rylant; Macmillan, 1995.

How Many Days to My Birthday? by Gus Clarke; Lothrop, Lee & Shepard, 1992.

The Jolly Postman by Janet and Allan Ahlberg; Little, Brown, 1986.

The Lettuce Leaf Birthday Letter by Linda Taylor; Dial Books for Young Readers, 1995.

On the Day You Were Born by Debra Frasier; Harcourt Brace Jovanovich, 1991.

Pablo's Tree by Pat Mora; Macmillan, 1994.

Some Birthday by Patricia Polacco; Simon & Schuster Books for Young Readers, 1991.

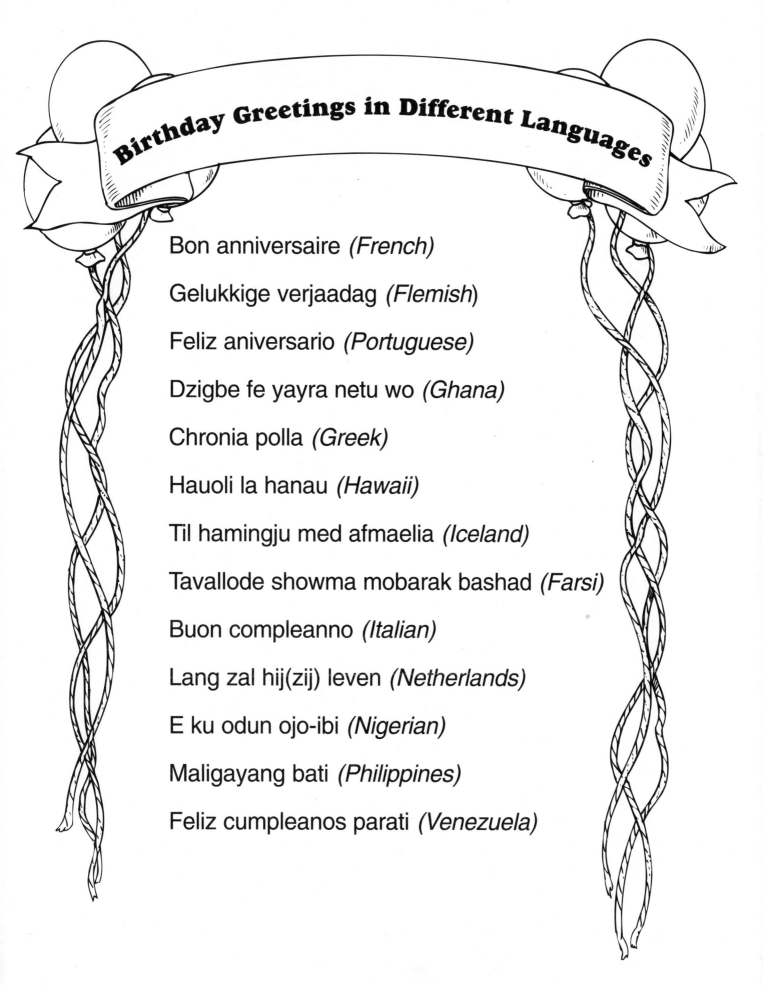

Birthday Greetings in Different Languages

Bon anniversaire *(French)*

Gelukkige verjaadag *(Flemish)*

Feliz aniversario *(Portuguese)*

Dzigbe fe yayra netu wo *(Ghana)*

Chronia polla *(Greek)*

Hauoli la hanau *(Hawaii)*

Til hamingju med afmaelia *(Iceland)*

Tavallode showma mobarak bashad *(Farsi)*

Buon compleanno *(Italian)*

Lang zal hij(zij) leven *(Netherlands)*

E ku odun ojo-ibi *(Nigerian)*

Maligayang bati *(Philippines)*

Feliz cumpleanos parati *(Venezuela)*

Our Birthday Book

A Class Book

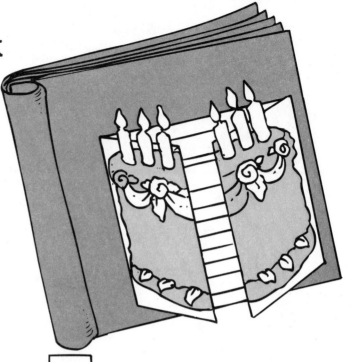

Materials

- reproducible forms on page 153
- 5" x 12" (13 x 30.5 cm) white construction paper
- 8" x 9" (20 x 23 cm) blue construction paper
- felt pens or crayons
- scissors, glue
- hole punch and ribbon

1

Fold the sides of the white construction paper to the center. Glue the form in the inside.

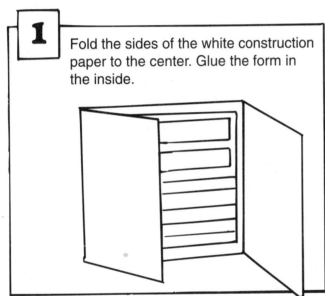

2

Color and cut out the cake form. Cut it down the center. Glue the cake on the cover of the white paper.

Glue the folded form to the blue paper. Add candles to the cake.

3

Put student papers together. Punch two holes on the left hand side. Secure with a ribbon and bow.

Writing Suggestions

Make a class book of birthdays.

My name is:

My birthday is:

My special talent is: _____

_____

_____

_____

_____

How to Make Books with Children EMC 578

Celebrate the Seasons

The seasons are caused by the tilting of the Earth on its axis as it rotates around the sun. The amount of sunlight hitting various parts of the Earth's surface changes from season to season. The seasons are reversed from northern to southern hemispheres. The explanations below are for the northern hemisphere.

Spring

On the first day of spring (the vernal or spring equinox) the sun is directly over the equator. Day and night are about the same length. The first day of each season varies by a day or two from year to year. The first day of spring is about March 21.

Summer

The first day of summer is called the summer solstice. On this day, the northern hemisphere is tilted its closest to the sun; the sun is overhead at the Tropic of Cancer. The first day of summer is about June 21.

Autumn

The first day of autumn (the autumnal equinox) the sun is again directly over the equator. Day and night are about the same length. The first day of autumn is about September 21.

Winter

The first day of winter is called the winter solstice. On this day, the northern hemisphere is tilted its farthest away from the sun; the sun is overhead at the Tropic of Capricorn. The first day of winter is about December 21.

Books to Read

Molly's Seasons by Ellen Kandoian; Dutton, 1992.

Why Do We Have Different Seasons? by Isaac Asimov; G. Stevens Children's Books, 1991.

Can't Sit Still by Karen E. Lotz; Dutton Children's Books, 1993.

How Does the Wind Walk? by Nancy While Carlstrom; Macmillan, 1993.

My Favorite Time of Year by Susan Pearson; Harper & Row, 1988.

The All Season Pop-Up

An Individual Student Book

Materials

- 4 copies of the pop-up form on page 156
- seasonal signs on page 157
- paper for cutting out original designs
- 9" x 12" (23 x 30.5 cm) construction paper
- crayons or felt pens
- scissors, glue

1 Fold and cut the pop-up forms.

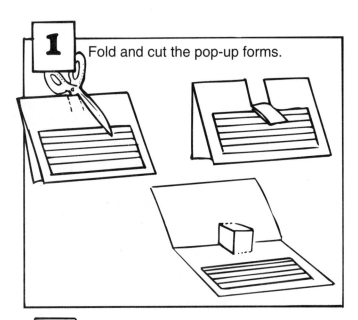

2 Glue the seasonal sign onto the tab. Decorate the background to fit the season. Use paper cut outs, crayons or felt pens.

3 Glue the pop-ups back-to-back. Fold the construction paper in half. Glue the pop-ups inside. (See pop-up hints, page 3)

Writing Suggestions

As the follow-up to a study of the changing seasons, write about:

> how the seasons are caused,
> characteristics of each season,
> activities for each season,
> the joys of each season, etc.

As a year-end activity, brainstorm (or refer to your ongoing classroom logs) school events of the year. Have your students choose a memorable event from each season and write about them.

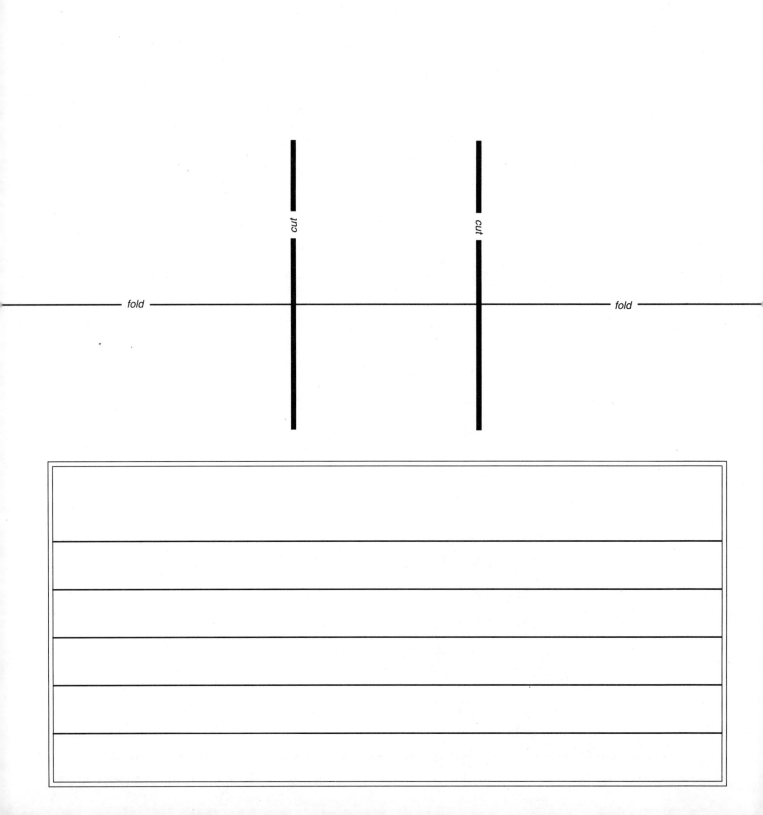

winter

spring

summer

autumn

How to Make Books with Children EMC 578

Our Calendar

Background

The calendar plays an important part in every classroom. Make a classroom calendar and use it to record personal celebrations and special days...Joey's birthday...Our first Spelling Test...Field Trip to the Pumpkin Farm...Amy lost a tooth...Carl broke his arm. You may want to include traditional holidays as well. At the end of the year, this calendar will be an exciting diary of special days gone by.

Books to Read

The Months of the Year by Paul Hughes; Garrett Educational Corporation, 1989.

Keeping Time by Franklyn M. Branley; Houghton Mifflin, 1993.

Time and the Seasons by Bobbie Kalman and Susan Hughes; Crabtree Publishing Company, 1986.

Calendar Art by Leonard Everett Fisher; Macmillan, 1987.

Facts

• Our calendar is based on the Gregorian Calendar. It was first introduced by Pope Gregory in 1583.

• The names of our months come mainly from the Romans. Most were named after Roman gods or goddesses, although a few come from Latin words.

• Some countries base religious celebrations on different calendars.The Moslem year is twelve lunar months of 29 or 30 days each. The Jewish year is twleve lunar months with an extra month added seven times every nineteen years.

 How to Make Books with Children EMC 578

My Own Calendar Book

An Individual Student Book

Materials

- 12 copies of the calendar face on page 160
- 9" x 12" (23 x 30.5 cm) construction paper
- pencils and crayons
- hole punch and yarn
- glue

1 Fill in the names and dates for each month.

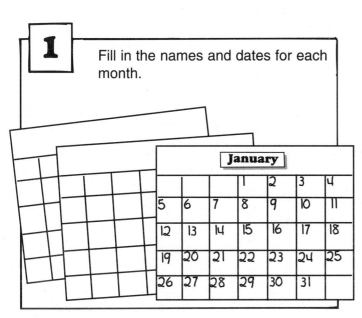

2 Place all the months in order. Staple the twelve calendar pages to the construction paper.

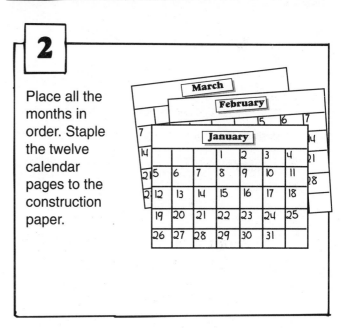

3 Write a short message each day to tell about important events.

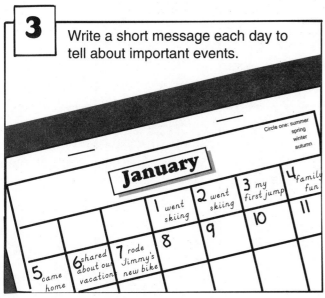

Writing Suggestions

This individual calendar can be used for personal or school entries.
It's an ideal place to record daily school activities and learnings.

glue here

Circle one: summer
spring
autumn
winter
